HEALING AND REPARENTING YOUR INNER CHILD

OVERCOMING NEGATIVE THOUGHT PATTERNS, BUILDING EMOTIONAL RESILIENCE, AND CULTIVATING SELF-LOVE WITH CBT AND OTHER PROVEN STRATEGIES

ALEXANDER KNIGHT

CONTENTS

INTRODUCTION

One evening, not too long ago, I found myself sitting alone in my living room, surrounded by the quiet hum of a world that seemed to have moved on without me. The weight of years of unresolved pain weighed heavy on my chest. I had just experienced an emotional breakdown that had been triggered by, what had seemed at the time to be, just a silly disagreement. But as I sat there, tears streaming down my face, I realized that this was not about the argument, the words which had been exchanged, at all. It was about something much deeper, something rooted in my past.

That night, I had a revelation. I needed to heal the child within me —the part of me that had been wounded, neglected, and misunderstood for so long. This was the moment that set me on a path of healing and reparenting my inner child.

But what exactly do we mean by the inner child? It represents the part of us that experienced – that went through all the highs and lows of childhood. This includes all our memories, experiences, and emotions from those early years. It is the core of our emotional and psychological well-being. When this inner child is wounded, it can lead to negative thought patterns and behaviors in our adult lives. Healing this part of ourselves is crucial for building emotional resilience and, well, to put it simply, just living happily.

The purpose of this book is to help you heal – pure and simple; to overcome negativity, and build emotional resilience through the recognition and then reformulation of childhood trauma. My vision is to offer a compassionate and practical guide that integrates proven therapeutic methods like Cognitive Behavioral Therapy (CBT), mindfulness, and practices to ensure self-compassion. Through these approaches, you will gain the tools to address emotional wounds, manage triggers, and foster deeper self-awareness.

So, what can you expect to gain from this book? In a nutshell, it'll offer a range of practical exercises, tools for emotional regulation, techniques for building self-love, and methods for managing triggers. These strategies are actionable and effective, designed to help you create lasting change in your life.

The book is divided into several sections. We'll start by understanding the concept of the inner child and its impact on our lives. Then, we will move on to explore various therapeutic methods and how they can be applied to healing. Each chapter will include exercises that you can bring to real world situations and relatable examples to help you apply these concepts to your own daily lived experience. This structure will guide you, step-by-step, through your healing journey.

Self-compassion and self-awareness are central themes throughout this book. They are essential for overcoming childhood trauma. By developing these essential aspects, you will learn to treat yourself with kindness and understanding. This will empower you to break free from negative cognitive distortions and reclaim your emotional freedom.

As mentioned, you'll find a bunch of personal stories and relatable examples as you read through. These stories will help you see yourself in the healing journey and understand the practical application of the concepts discussed. They will bring the material to life and make it more accessible.

Anyway, allow me to introduce myself. I am Alexander Knight, a holistic wellness coach and author with over two decades of experience. My work focuses on emotional healing and personal growth. I aim to make complex ideas approachable and easy to apply. My approach is compassionate and insightful, designed to help you unlock your fullest potential.

As you embark on this journey with me, I want to assure you, from a deeply personal perspective, that change is possible. With the tools and strategies provided in this book – developed over decades of experience, you can overcome the limitations imposed by unresolved trauma. You can create lasting change and reclaim your emotional freedom.

So, Dear reader, I invite you to take this journey with me. Let us heal together, build emotional resilience, and cultivate self-love. The path to healing and reparenting your inner child lies ahead, and it is a journey where every single step is worth taking.

1

UNDERSTANDING YOUR INNER CHILD

G rowing up, I often felt a deep sense of loneliness, even when surrounded by family or friends – this was a particular strong feeling during adolescence, but even during adulthood, it has tended to linger more than I would like to admit. There were moments when I couldn't understand why I felt so disconnected and misunderstood. It wasn't until much later in life, during an intense therapy session, that I began to realize these feelings were remnants of my inner child crying out for attention and healing. This revelation was a turning point for me, opening the door to understanding the profound impact of the inner child on my emotional and psychological well-being.

1.1 THE CONCEPT OF THE INNER CHILD

The inner child represents the childlike aspect of your personality, encompassing your behaviors, memories, and emotions from childhood. This part of you holds both the innocence and wonder of your early years, as well as the wounds and traumas you may have experienced. In psychological terms, the inner child is a critical component of your psyche, influencing your thoughts, reactions, and overall emotional health. The origins of this concept can be traced back to Carl Jung, a pioneering Swiss psychologist – active during the early to mid-20th century, who introduced the idea of the "child archetype." To put it simply, Jung believed that the inner child – this "child archetype" - holds your childhood experiences and emotions, which shape your adult personality.

Understanding how the inner child can affect aspects of your life is fundamental. When this part of you is ignored or neglected, it can lead to unresolved trauma, negative patterns, and maladaptive coping mechanisms. For instance, you might find yourself overreacting to minor setbacks or feeling inexplicable sadness or anger. These are often signs that your inner child is influencing your emotional responses – taking the reins and leading you by the limited knowledge it has of the world. Let's focus on how acknowledging and healing your inner child can foster a sense of self-compassion and emotional resilience, essential for overcoming past traumas.

Historically, the concept of the inner child has evolved through the contributions of several key psychologists. Carl Jung's work laid the foundation, but it was Alice Miller, another Swiss psychologist, who expanded on this idea in her groundbreaking books such as *The Drama of the Gifted Child* and *The Body Never Lies*. Miller emphasized that childhood trauma is stored in the body and that acknowledging and addressing these early wounds is crucial for emotional healing. Her work has influenced many therapists and continues to be a cornerstone in understanding the long-term effects of childhood trauma.

Today, modern interpretations of the inner child integrate various therapeutic approaches, making the concept more accessible and applicable. Therapies such as Cognitive Behavioral Therapy (CBT), mindfulness practices, and regression therapy have been shown to be effective ways to allow us to heal the inner child. These methods provide practical tools for addressing emotional wounds and bringing about greater self-awareness.

The role of the inner child in our daily lives is profound. It influences our behaviors, emotional responses, and decision-making processes. For example, you might find yourself struggling with low self-esteem or engaging in people-pleasing behaviors to seek validation, often rooted in childhood experiences of neglect or criticism. The inner child can also impact your relationships, leading to trust issues or difficulty setting boundaries. By recognizing these influences, you can begin to address and heal the underlying wounds, transforming your emotional responses and behaviors.

In popular culture, the concept of the inner child has been depicted in various forms, making it more relatable and easier to understand. Movies and literature often explore themes of childhood trauma and healing, resonating with audiences on a deep emotional level. Films like *Good Will Hunting* delve into the complexities of childhood experiences and their lasting impact on adult life, where films like *Inside Out* show some of the processes which go into the very formation of these traumas and how they are likely to be carried forward into adulthood. Quotes from influential figures, such as Carl Jung's "In every adult, there lurks a child—an eternal child, something that is always becoming, is never completed, and calls for unceasing care, attention, and education," highlight the importance of nurturing our child within.

In this book, you'll see that understanding must give way to acknowledging. By going through this process, we speak directly to this part of yourself and address the emotional wounds you hold. Then, you can begin to cultivate self-compassion, build emotional resilience, and reclaim your emotional freedom. As you read, remember to take a moment's respite and reflect on what is being said and how this can relate to your own lived experience.

1.2 HOW CHILDHOOD TRAUMA AFFECTS ADULTHOOD

Let's take a look at just how unresolved childhood trauma can manifest in various ways, deeply affecting our behavior when we are adults and the emotional states that we find ourselves in. Take, for instance, the story of Emily, a successful professional in her mid-thirties. Despite her achievements, Emily struggles with trust issues in her personal relationships. She often finds herself questioning the intentions of close friends and partners, leading to frequent conflicts and emotional isolation. This distrust stems from her childhood experiences of emotional neglect, where her feelings were dismissed, and her needs were overlooked. These early wounds have left a lasting imprint, causing her to build walls to try to protect herself – lock herself away somewhere safe; yet, these same walls keep genuine connections at bay. If we do not make efforts to fix such inner turmoil, we end up becoming like a *Selfish Giant* – like Oscar Wilde depicts in his story of the same name. And, just like in this story, if we block people out, our garden will not flourish.

Similarly, consider the case of Michael, who deals with persistent anxiety. As a child, Michael witnessed domestic violence, leaving him in a constant state of alertness. This hypervigilance followed him into adulthood, manifesting as a chronic condition whereby his thoughts are allowed to unnecessarily race – planning constantly for disaster. Simple daily tasks, like attending a social gathering or speaking in front of colleagues, trigger intense fear and panic. Michael's past trauma has wired his brain to perceive threats even in safe environments, making it difficult for him to feel at ease. What start as ways for the brain to protect us in childhood become restrictions in adulthood.

Childhood trauma can take many forms, each with possible long-term effects. Emotional neglect, for instance, occurs when a child's emotional needs are consistently ignored or dismissed. This can lead to low self-esteem, difficulty expressing emotions, and a constant need for validation in adulthood. Physical abuse, on the other hand, inflicts both physical and emotional scars. Adults who experienced physical abuse as children may struggle with trust issues, fear of authority figures, and recurring nightmares or flashbacks.

Witnessing domestic violence is another form of trauma that can leave deep psychological wounds. Children who grow up in violent households often feel powerless and fearful, which can translate into anxiety, depression, and relationship issues in later life. The loss of a parent or caregiver, whether through death, abandonment, or separation, is a profound hardship that can lead to attachment issues, fear of abandonment, and depression.

Symptoms of unresolved trauma are varied but often interlinked. Chronic feelings of shame or guilt are common. You might find yourself ruminating over past mistakes or feeling unworthy of love and happiness. Forming healthy relationships can become a significant challenge, as past traumas can make it difficult to trust others or feel secure in intimate connections, as well as maybe feeling like you are undeserving of love and connection. Persistent anxiety or depression is another hallmark of unresolved trauma. You may experience constant worry, panic attacks, or a pervasive sense of sadness that seems impossible to shake. Self-sabotaging behaviors, such as procrastination, substance abuse, or pushing away loved ones, are coping mechanisms common to such crises. These behaviors often stem from a deep-seated belief that one does not deserve success or happiness.

Let's take a look at Sarah. She grew up in a household where emotional abuse was a daily occurrence. Her father's harsh words and constant criticism left her with a deep sense of worthlessness. As an adult, Sarah found it difficult to assert herself at work, often downplaying her achievements and avoiding opportunities for advancement. It wasn't until she began therapy and confronted her childhood experiences that she started to reclaim her self-worth and pursue her career ambitions with a passion more befitting the person she truly is.

Mark's experience illustrates the long-term impact of childhood neglect. Raised by a single parent who was often absent, Mark learned to fend for himself from a young age. This early independence masked a deep sense of abandonment. In his adult relationships, Mark struggled with dependency and fear of rejection. He would either cling too tightly to partners or push them away before they could leave him. Understanding and addressing his childhood neglect allowed Mark to develop healthier, more balanced relationships.

The key takeaway here is that trauma casts long shadows over adulthood, influencing behaviors, emotions, and relationships – it's something that we'll come back to again and again in the book as we formulate ways to best respond to it. By addressing the wounds of the past, whether through therapy, self-compassion practices, or other healing methods, it is possible to break free from these negative patterns. Let's investigate some of the clues which might indicate we too our experiencing something similar to Emily, Michael, Sarah or Mark.

1.3 RECOGNIZING THE SIGNS OF A WOUNDED INNER CHILD

When I began to fully understand the concept of the inner child, it became clear that my own childhood wounds were still very much extant in my adult behaviors. Over time though, I learned to recognize these signs, which are often subtle, yet which pervade large swathes of our lived experience. One notable behavioral indicator for me was overreacting to minor setbacks. Picture a day when a small error I made at work leads me to feel a disproportionate sense of failure and self-criticism. I learned that such a reaction often stems from a wounded inner child who was perhaps reprimanded harshly for mistakes in the past. These overreactions are not about the present situation but are echoes of unresolved childhood emotions.

Another significant indicator is the fear of abandonment. This fear can manifest in various ways, such as clinging to people – who may not always be worth your efforts - or pushing people away at the slightest hint of conflict. Imagine feeling an intense need to constantly check in with a partner or friend, fearing that any lapse in communication signifies a loss of affection. This behavior often has roots in early experiences of neglect or loss, where the inner child learned to equate abandonment with silence or even absence. This fear can create a cycle of insecurity and dependency, making it difficult to form healthy, balanced relationships.

Difficulty trusting others is another common behavioral sign of an emotional wound. If you find yourself questioning the motives of friends or partners, suspecting betrayal even when there's no evidence, it could be that you are reacting to past betrayals or broken promises. This lack of trust can lead to isolation and loneliness as the inner child tries to protect itself from further hurt – pushing away rather than learning to embrace. Similarly, self-critical thoughts are a hallmark. These thoughts often manifest as an internal dialogue filled with harsh judgments and negative self-talk. You might find yourself thinking, "I'm not good enough," or "I always mess things up," reflecting the critical voices from your past.

Emotionally, a wounded inner child can cause chronic feelings of sadness or emptiness. These feelings may not have an obvious trigger and can linger despite external successes or positive experiences. This emotional state often reflects unresolved grief or unmet emotional needs from childhood. Intense feelings of anger or rage are also a factor. You might find yourself reacting with disproportionate anger to situations that seem trivial to others. This anger is often a defense mechanism, masking deeper feelings of hurt or vulnerability that were never truly addressed.

How about persistent fear or anxiety? This too can manifest as a constant sense of dread or worry about the future, even when things are going well. The inner child, conditioned by past traumas, remains in a heightened state of alertness, always anticipating danger. These emotional signs are not just psychological; they can have physical manifestations as well. Chronic fatigue is one such symptom. Despite getting enough sleep, you might feel constantly drained, a reflection of the emotional burden you have by carrying on you this extra individual – this childhood you, bent on transforming your present to suit their whims. Unexplained aches and pains are another physical indicator. These can occur without any medical explanation, often linked to the mind needing to project onto the body the anguish that it exudes. A compromised immune system, resulting from chronic stress and emotional turmoil, can make you more susceptible to infections and illnesses – another possible vicious circle.

Recognizing these signs is the first step toward healing, but how do you assess the state of your inner child? Self-assessment quizzes can be a useful tool. These quizzes, designed to help you reflect on your behaviors, emotions, and physical symptoms, can provide insights into the areas that need attention. Journaling prompts for self-reflection are another effective method. Writing about your childhood experiences, your current emotional state, and your reactions to various situations can help you identify patterns and triggers.

For instance, a prompt like: "Describe a recent situation where you felt intense anger. What memories or feelings did it evoke?" can help you uncover the roots of your emotional reactions. These tools are not just about identifying problems but also about understanding and addressing them. By regularly engaging in self-assessment and reflection, you can begin to heal your wounded inner child, fostering a sense of self-compassion and emotional resilience that will transform your life.

Here is a list of some common prompts which I'd recommend that you find the time to work through:

1. Describe a recent situation where you felt intense anger. What memories or feelings did it evoke?
2. Recall a recent moment when you felt overwhelmed by sadness. What memories or experiences from your childhood does this sadness remind you of?
3. Think of a time you felt an intense sense of fear or anxiety. What childhood events or feelings does this reaction bring to mind?
4. Describe a situation where you felt an unexpected wave of jealousy. How does this emotion connect to your early experiences with relationships or self-worth?

5. Reflect on a moment when you felt a strong sense of rejection or abandonment. What past experiences, particularly from your childhood, does this trigger for you?

6. Identify a recent experience that filled you with deep disappointment. What past situations or unmet expectations from your childhood does this feeling relate to?

7. Think back to a time when you felt the urge to please others at your own expense. How do your childhood experiences influence this need for approval?

8. Recall a situation where you felt a surge of frustration. What memories or feelings from your childhood does this frustration evoke, and why?

9. Describe an instance where you felt a strong sense of shame. How does this shame connect to experiences or messages you received during your childhood?

10. Consider a recent moment when you experienced a profound sense of joy or happiness. How does this joy contrast with your childhood experiences, and what does it reveal about your inner child?

Answering these honestly will start to give you a sense of where you at in terms of your emotional state.

1.4 THE SCIENCE BEHIND INNER CHILD HEALING

The process that goes into this deep healing can be both enlightening and empowering. At the heart of this process is the concept of neuroplasticity, the brain's remarkable ability to change and adapt throughout our lives. It allows the brain to form new neural connections, reorganize itself, and even compensate for injuries or diseases. This adaptability is crucial for healing the inner child because it means that, with the right interventions, we can rewire our brain to overcome past traumas and develop healthier emotional and psychological patterns.

Let's take a look at this in action. When someone engages in therapy, the brain begins to change in response to the new experiences and insights that arise during sessions. For instance, Cognitive Behavioral Therapy (CBT) helps individuals challenge and reframe negative thought patterns. Over time, these new, healthier ways of thinking become ingrained, effectively rewiring the brain. Similarly, mindfulness practices promote changes in brain regions associated with attention, emotional regulation, and self-awareness. These changes demonstrate the brain's capacity to adapt and heal, offering hope to anyone struggling with the scars of childhood trauma. This is in harsh contrast to previous models that suggested the brain, after adolescence is essentially like a fixed lump. Fortunately, science has disproved such notions and we can all benefit from knowing that the brain in fact operates in an entirely *plastic* way.

Mindfulness-Based Stress Reduction (MBSR) is another powerful therapeutic approach. It involves practices like meditation and mindful breathing to cultivate present-moment awareness and reduce stress. By regularly engaging in mindfulness practices, you train your brain to become more attuned to your thoughts and emotions without judgment. This heightened awareness helps you break free from automatic reactions driven by past traumas, allowing you to respond to situations with greater clarity and calmness.

Regression therapy is particularly effective too. It involves guided sessions where you revisit past experiences to uncover and process unresolved emotions. By addressing these deeply-buried emotions, you can release their hold on the present, paving the way for emotional healing and growth. This type of therapy often includes techniques like guided visualization and inner child dialogues, which help you to connect with and nurture your wounded inner child.

Scientific research very much supports the effectiveness of these therapeutic approaches. Studies on CBT, to take one example, have consistently shown its efficacy in treating a range of emotional and psychological issues, including those stemming from childhood trauma. Research indicates that CBT not only reduces symptoms of anxiety and depression but also promotes long-term positive changes in brain function and structure – again, thanks to the plasticity that we all have at our disposal. Similarly, mindfulness practices have been extensively studied, with evidence showing their benefits in enhancing emotional regulation, reducing stress, and improving overall well-being.

One inspiring case is that of Jane, who struggled with severe anxiety rooted in childhood trauma. Through a combination of CBT and mindfulness practices, she learned to identify and challenge her negative thought patterns. Over time, she noticed significant improvements in her anxiety levels and overall emotional health. Jane's story illustrates how these therapeutic approaches can facilitate profound healing and transformation.

Another success story is Michael, who experienced a breakthrough with regression therapy. He had long struggled with feelings of abandonment and low self-worth due to a harsh childhood. During regression sessions, Michael was able to reconnect with his younger self, offering the compassion and validation he had missed. This process allowed him to heal deep-seated wounds and develop a more positive self-image.

These stories highlight the transformative power of therapeutic approaches in healing the inner child. By leveraging the brain's neuroplasticity, these methods offer practical and effective tools for overcoming past traumas and building a healthier, more resilient self. In your healing journey, it's essential to remember that the brain's capacity for change is limitless. The tools and strategies discussed in this book are designed to help you tap into this potential, offering a pathway to healing and emotional freedom. By embracing these therapeutic approaches, you can create lasting change, overcome the limitations imposed by unresolved trauma, and reclaim your emotional well-being.

2

CULTIVATING SELF-COMPASSION AND SELF-LOVE

One morning, as the sun began to peek through my bedroom curtains, I awoke, dragging myself into the bathroom. I found myself staring into the mirror, completely overwhelmed by a sense of inadequacy. I had just faced another sleepless night, riddled with self-critical thoughts about not being good enough at work or how I constantly fail to maintain healthy relationships. The reflection staring back at me was a person who desperately needed kindness but received only harsh judgment. It was in that quiet, vulnerable moment that I realized the missing piece in my healing was self-compassion. This revelation was a turning point, leading me to understand that treating myself with the same kindness I would offer a friend, or even a stranger, was not just beneficial—it was entirely necessary in order to overcome this myriad of negative feelings.

2.1 THE IMPORTANCE OF SELF-COMPASSION

Self-compassion is a powerful concept that simply asks the question: How can extend the kindness that I normally lavish on others and direct it inwardly – for myself? At its core, self-compassion is about being gentle with yourself, especially when you face challenges or make mistakes. It consists of three main components: self-kindness, common humanity, and mindfulness. Let's take a little look at each of these. Self-kindness involves treating oneself with warmth and understanding rather than being harshly critical. Common humanity, however, involves recognizing that suffering, and personal inadequacy, are part of the shared human experience, not something that isolates you from others, but something which unites you. Mindfulness, as we mentioned previously and will come back to frequently, requires taking a balanced approach to negative emotions so that feelings are neither suppressed nor exaggerated. Unlike self-esteem, which often relies on comparing yourself to others and can lead to narcissism or a fragile sense of self-worth, self-compassion is a stable source of support and resilience.

The benefits of practicing self-compassion are profound and well-supported by scientific research. One of the most significant psychological benefits is the reduction of anxiety and depression. When you practice self-compassion, you activate the brain's care-giving system, which releases oxytocin, a hormone that promotes feelings of love and bonding. This reduces the stress hormone cortisol, leading to lower levels of anxiety and depression overall. Another key benefit is increased emotional resilience. Self-compassion helps you bounce back from setbacks more quickly because you're able to directly soothe yourself and maintain a balanced perspective – one that you alone work to conceive. This resilience is crucial for navigating life's challenges without becoming overwhelmed. Additionally, self-compassion enhances overall well-being. People who practice self-compassion report higher levels of happiness, optimism, and life satisfaction. They are also more likely to engage in healthy behaviors, such as eating well, exercising regularly, and getting enough sleep, which further contributes to their overall levels of contentedness.

There are several common misconceptions about self-compassion that need to be addressed though. One major misconception is that self-compassion is equivalent to self-pity. This couldn't be further from the truth and it's important to disabuse ourselves of such a notion. Wallowing in our problems is really not what we've talking about here; it's about acknowledging your pain and responding to it with kindness and understanding. Another misconception is that self-compassion leads to complacency. Some people fear that if they are too kind to themselves, they will lose their motivation to improve. However, research shows that self-compassion actually fosters accountability and growth. When you treat yourself with kindness, you feel more secure and are more willing to take more risks and try new things because you're not paralyzed by the fear of failure. Finally, some believe that self-compassion is a form of self-indulgence. They worry that being kind to themselves means letting themselves off the hook too easily. In reality, self-compassion involves taking responsibility for your actions and recognizing that you are worthy of care and respect, even when you make mistakes.

Consider the story of Lisa, a high-achieving professional who constantly berated herself for any perceived failure. Lisa's self-criticism led to chronic stress and burnout. After learning about self-compassion, she began practicing self-kindness and mindfulness. She started speaking to herself as she would to a close friend, with encouragement and understanding. This shift transformed her life. Lisa's stress levels decreased, and she found renewed energy and passion for her work. Her relationships also improved as she became more patient and empathetic, both with herself and others.

Another inspiring case is that of John, who struggled with depression for years. John had internalized a harsh inner critic from his childhood, which perpetuated and fed back to him these feelings of worthlessness. Through therapy, John was introduced to self-compassion practices. He learned to recognize when his inner critic was taking over and to respond with positive and compassionate self-talk. This practice significantly improved his mental health. John reported feeling more hopeful and connected to others, realizing that his struggles were part of the human experience, not a personal failing. By embracing such feelings, John found the strength to pursue his passions and build a more fulfilling life.

Self-compassion is not just something that is nice to have, like a piece of jewelry; it's a crucial component of healing and emotional resilience. By practicing self-compassion, you can transform your relationship with yourself, reduce anxiety and depression, and cultivate a more balanced, fulfilling life.

2.2 DAILY AFFIRMATIONS FOR SELF-LOVE

Let's dig a little deeper how we can begin to cultivate self-compassion. Creating effective daily affirmations for self-love is one powerful way to transform how you perceive yourself. The key to crafting affirmations lies in using positive language and the present tense. This helps reinforce a sense of immediacy and reality. Start by identifying areas where you seek improvement or healing. Write affirmations that reflect these goals in a positive light. For example, instead of saying "I will not be anxious," say "I am calm and at peace." Use constructive language that focuses on what you want to achieve, rather than what you want to avoid. This shift in phrasing can make a significant difference in how your mind processes these statements. Personalize your affirmations to resonate with your unique experiences and aspirations. This is guaranteed to make them more meaningful and impactful.

Integrating affirmations into your daily routine can be a great way to make them stick. Consistency is crucial, as repetition helps ingrain these positive statements into your subconscious mind. Begin your day with a morning routine that includes these affirmations. You don't have to start big – just begin with something simple and work around them based on how you feel. Upon waking, for example, take a few moments to repeat your affirmations aloud. This sets a positive tone for the day and reinforces your commitment to self-love. Another effective method is to use sticky notes or affirmation apps. Place sticky notes with your affirmations around your home or workspace, where you will see them frequently. This constant visual reminder helps keep your affirmations at the forefront of your mind. Speaking affirmations aloud during daily activities, such as while brushing your teeth or during your commute, can also reinforce their impact. The key is to integrate them seamlessly into your routine, making them a natural part of your day.

Self-love affirmations can serve as a great starting point as they are quick, simple and effective. Here are a few you might find helpful: "I am worthy of love and respect," "I am enough just as I am," and "I choose to be kind to myself today." These affirmations cover various aspects of self-love and self-worth, helping you to build a more positive perception of yourself. You can tailor these examples to suit your specific needs and experiences. For instance, if you struggle with self-doubt, you might say, "I trust in my abilities and judgment." If you find it hard to prioritize self-care, an affirmation like "I deserve to take time for myself" can be empowering. The goal is to create affirmations that speak to your inner needs and aspirations, fostering a sense of self-compassion and love.

Remember, it's always a good idea to track the impact of your affirmations on your self-perception and emotional state. One effective way to do this is through journaling. Keep a journal where you write down your affirmations and reflect on how they make you feel. Note any changes in your thoughts, emotions, and behaviors over time. You might consider starting with a prompt like, "How do I feel about myself today compared to a week ago?" This helps you to track your progress and think more deeply about your patterns of thinking attributed to various scenarios. Self-reflection exercises can also be beneficial. Set aside time each week to reflect on your journey with affirmations. Ask yourself questions like, "What positive changes have I noticed?" and "How have my affirmations influenced my self-perception?" This practice not only reinforces the impact of your affirmations but also helps you stay more motivated and committed to your journey of self-love.

2.3 MEDITATIONS FOR GREATER SELF-COMPASSION

These are an incredibly powerful tool for emotional healing, allowing you to cultivate kindness and understanding towards yourself. These meditations involve focusing inwardly, acknowledging your pain, and responding with nurturing care. The purpose of self-compassion meditations is to help you develop a gentler, more supportive relationship with yourself. By regularly practicing these meditations, you can enhance your emotional regulation and self-awareness, which are crucial for overcoming past traumas and building resilience. Regular practice is key, as it helps reinforce the neural pathways associated with self-compassion, making it easier to access these feelings even during challenging times.

One of the most effective self-compassion meditations is the loving-kindness meditation. This practice involves sitting comfortably, closing your eyes, and directing kind and loving thoughts towards yourself. Begin by silently repeating phrases like, "May I be happy, may I be healthy, may I be safe, may I live with ease." Allow these words to resonate deeply within you, filling you with a sense of warmth and kindness. As you become more comfortable with this practice, you can extend these wishes to others, starting with loved ones and then including individuals who you want to wish well. This meditation nurtures self-compassion while also deepening your empathy and strengthening your connections with others.

Another powerful technique is the soothing touch meditation. This involves using physical touch to activate the body's parasympathetic nervous system (PNS), which can help make you feel calmer and promote feelings of safety and comfort. Start by placing the hand you write with over your heart, or just simple place that hand over your other. Close your eyes and take a few deep breaths, focusing on the sensation of your touch. Imagine that this touch is filled with love and compassion, soothing any pain or discomfort you may be feeling. This practice can be particularly helpful during moments of intense stress or emotional turmoil, providing an immediate sense of relief and grounding. The more you get accustomed to doing this, the quicker it becomes to jump into this state.

Creating a conducive environment for meditation is essential for maximizing its benefits. Find a quiet, comfortable space where you won't be disturbed. This could be a corner of a room, a cozy chair, or even a spot in your garden. Minimize distractions by turning off your phone, closing or locking the door, and informing others that you need some uninterrupted time. Consider adding elements that enhance the sense of tranquility, such as soft lighting, calming scents like lavender, incense sticks, and soothing background music. The goal is to create a sanctuary where you can fully relax and focus on your meditation practice.

Incorporating self-compassion meditations into your daily routine doesn't have to be complicated. Start with short sessions, perhaps five to ten minutes, and gradually increase the duration as you become more comfortable. You can combine meditation with daily activities to make it more accessible. For example, practice loving-kindness meditation during your morning walk or use the soothing touch technique while lying in bed before sleep. The key is to make these practices a regular part of your day, so they become second nature. Also, don't feel they have to be done alone. You can share many of these meditations with a loved one; the practice can even bring about a further personal connection with others.

By integrating these meditative practices0 into your life, you can cultivate a deeper sense of kindness and understanding towards yourself. These practices not only help heal emotional wounds, but also build a foundation of resilience and self-awareness that supports your overall well-being. It's only with practice and dedication that these feelings become intrinsic to your being; this is not a quick fix, so bear this in mind if you're a person who tends to look for quick fixes. The best thing is to reflect on how you feel as this will guide you forward, knowing whether to change it up by trying a new meditation or changing for how long or even where you do your practice.

2.4 OVERCOMING SELF-BLAME AND CRITICISM

Understanding just how we blame ourselves and how this can potentially lead to self-criticism involves recognizing its deep psychological roots. Often, these feelings originate in childhood experiences where you may have been unnecessarily held responsible for things that went wrong. This internalized guilt can carry into adulthood, manifesting as a constant, nagging voice that tells you you're at fault for every mishap. This pervasive self-blame can significantly impact your self-esteem and mental health, leading to feelings of inadequacy and depression. It's crucial to identify exactly when you are embarking on this route; notice it, and work out ways to avoid it in the future. For example, if you find yourself consistently attributing failures or setbacks to personal flaws rather than external factors, you are likely caught in the 'self-blame cycle'. This mindset not only diminishes your self-worth but also hinders your ability to see situations objectively and learn from them because of this. How are we ever going to truly learn if we don't have all the salient information in front of us?

To combat these feelings, you can employ several effective techniques. One of the most powerful methods is cognitive reframing. This involves identifying negative thought patterns and consciously shifting them to more positive and realistic ones. For instance, if you catch yourself thinking, "I'm terrible at my job because I made a mistake," try reframing it to, "Everyone makes mistakes; it's an opportunity to learn and improve." This shift in perspective can help you break free from the cycle of self-blame and foster a more balanced concept of your behaviors. Another practical technique is engaging in self-compassionate self-talk. Whenever you notice self-blame creeping in, pause and ask yourself what you would say to a friend in a similar situation. Chances are that you would offer them understanding and encouragement rather than the harsh criticism you've been leveling at yourself. Why not be just as kind to yourself, knowing that mistakes are a natural part of the human experience? Again, as we've mentioned, journaling exercises can also be incredibly beneficial. Take time each day to write about your experiences and emotions, focusing on reframing negative thoughts. Why not just spend 5 minutes each day logging a negative thought and then reframing it? This can be easily done by drawing a line down the center of a piece of paper – the left column represents the negative thought, where the right could be the reformulation of this.

Addressing self-criticism is closely linked to overcoming self-blame. The inner critic, that harsh, judgmental voice inside your head, often stems from the same roots as self-blame. It's essential to identify this inner critic and recognize its impact on your mental health. Self-critical thoughts can be debilitating, leading to feelings of worthlessness and despair. To challenge these thoughts, start by questioning their validity. Ask yourself, "Is this thought based on fact or just a negative perception?" Often, you'll find that self-critical thoughts are exaggerated or unfounded. It's actually incredible the thoughts we can attribute to ourselves that we would never apply to others, let along others apply them to us. Replace these criticisms with constructive feedback. Instead of thinking, "I always mess things up," try, "I made a mistake, but I can learn from this and do better next time." This shift not only reduces the power of the inner critic but also promotes a growth mindset.

Take the story of Maria, who grew up in a household where she was constantly blamed for her siblings' misbehavior. Her parent's thought that, as she was the oldest, she had to be responsible for them, but she herself was only a child. This feeling of being culpable stayed with her into adulthood, affecting her relationships and career negatively. Through therapy and self-compassion practices, Maria learned to recognize and challenge her self-blaming thoughts. She began using cognitive reframing and journaling to rewire her thinking. She told herself that it was unfair for her to continue this unnecessary judgment of herself, and that it certainly wouldn't have been the intention of those around her who love her, so why maintain something so detrimental?

Another inspiring case is that of David, who struggled with severe self-criticism for many years of adult life, simply due to the fact that he had a parent that was over-critical. Every time David made a mistake – whether at work, or at home, his inner critic would berate him, leading to anxiety and depression that kind of acted like tunnel-vision, in the sense that he couldn't see outside of this dark hole. By identifying this inner critic and practicing self-compassionate self-talk, David gradually reduced the power of these negative thoughts. Through practice, he basically could become hyper-aware of when the inner critic was active – like a cartoon devil on his shoulder. He replaced him with constructive feedback and focused on his strengths and achievements, for which he knew, deep down, that there were many – and many to come. This shift not only improved David's mental health but also enabled him to pursue his passions with confidence.

As we can see from these examples, overcoming these feelings can help us to better make sense of the world around us; enable us to better grasp our lived realities, and no longer find it necessary to dwell on the voice of the critic. Our process to achieve this can be summarized as such:

- Identify the roots of negative patterns.
- Use practical techniques to challenge and reframe these patterns.
- Develop a more compassionate and supportive inner dialogue.
- Boost emotional well-being and build resilience for life's challenges.

As you continue your journey of healing and self-discovery, remember everything we discuss here is a *process* – one thing follows another. The techniques and practices we've discussed in this chapter are powerful tools that will support you every step of the way, helping you build a stronger, more resilient self. In the next chapter, we will explore further practical exercises for healing, providing you with actionable strategies to make sure you stay clear and focused on your journey towards improved mental health.

3

PRACTICAL EXERCISES FOR HEALING

We've covered a number of techniques and practices already so far in this book, but let's delve deeper and try to focus on the specifics. As you read, keep thinking about how you can apply some of these techniques to your own daily lived experience; after all, this book is about you, and designing such strategies so they favor your own personal goals and aspirations.

3.1 JOURNALING PROMPTS FOR EMOTIONAL RELEASE

One evening, as I was sifting through old notebooks, I stumbled upon a journal entry from my teenage years – "The horror!" I thought, already feeling myself going red with embarrassment. As I read though, I saw how the words on the page were raw and unfiltered, filled with the angst and confusion of youth. There was something profoundly therapeutic about reading those words and I was certain there must have been too for the boy jotting them down. It dawned on me that journaling at that age had been a form of self-therapy, a silent witness to my struggles and triumphs.

Emotional journaling is a powerful practice that involves writing about your feelings and experiences to gain clarity and release pent-up emotions. The primary purpose of emotional journaling is to create a safe space where you can explore your innermost thoughts and feelings without judgment. This practice allows you to process complex emotions, identify patterns in your behavior, and gain insights into your emotional landscape. The act itself of writing itself can be cathartic, providing an outlet for emotions that might otherwise remain suppressed. According to research by the distinguished American psychologist James Pennebaker, whose work focuses on the connections between language and emotions, expressive writing can in fact improve how the immune system functions and reduce stress. Much of his work highlights the profound impact that journaling can have on both our mental and physical health.

Creating a consistent journaling routine is crucial for maximizing the benefits of this practice though. Start by setting aside a dedicated time each day for journaling. Whether it's first thing in the morning or just before bed, choose a time that fits in seamlessly. Consistency is key, as regular practice helps reinforce the habit and deepen your self-awareness. Find a quiet and comfortable space where you can write without interruptions. This could be a cozy corner in your home, a quiet park, or even a favorite café. Using prompts can help you get started and provide direction for your writing. Prompts serve as a guide, helping you focus on specific aspects of your emotional experience.

To facilitate emotional release, here are a variety of journaling prompts designed to cover different emotional experiences. First, consider writing about a time you felt deeply hurt and how it affected you. This prompt encourages you to confront and process painful memories, helping you to diffuse the emotional charge associated with them. Another useful prompt is to describe your happiest childhood memory and why it stands out. Reflecting on positive experiences can provide a sense of comfort and remind you of the joy that exists. Why do only have to write about negative things? Additionally, writing about what you are most grateful for today can shift your focus to positive aspects of your life, offering a sense of gratitude and well-being. Finally, detail a recent event that triggered strong emotions and explore why it happened this way. This prompt helps you identify and understand your triggers, providing insights into your emotional responses and how to manage them better. Who knows? You may not have even given thought to these things, and they may have just sat there, simmering away, affecting how you go about handling the present.

To deepen your journaling practice, consider using stream-of-consciousness writing. This technique involves writing continuously without censoring your thoughts, allowing your subconscious mind to flow freely onto the page. Many famous authors have used this technique in their writing, especially throughout the 20th century. One reason they did this is because this style of writing can reveal hidden emotions and insights that structured writing might miss. Reflecting on past journal entries is another powerful strategy. Regularly review your previous entries to identify patterns, track your progress, and gain new perspectives on your experiences. Journaling alongside other therapeutic practices can also enhance its effectiveness. For instance, you might write after a mindfulness meditation session to help the creative juices flow.

Emotional journaling is a versatile and accessible tool that can significantly aid in your healing process. By establishing a consistent routine, using prompts to guide your writing, and employing strategies to deepen your practice, you can harness the full potential of journaling. Think of your journal as your trusted companion; take them everywhere, let them see the world as you see it, dedicate time to them, but sometimes give them space, like we would for any companion.

3.2 VISUALIZATION TECHNIQUES

This idea works through accessing emotional wounds and challenging them by creating positive mental imagery. It involves using your imagination to conjure up vivid, calming images in your mind, which can reduce stress and improve your mental health. This technique is grounded in the idea that the brain responds to imagined experiences in ways that are similar to real ones – kind of like a vivid dream. By engaging your senses and inner self-talk, visualization can help you reshape your emotional landscape, making it an effective method for overcoming trauma, anxiety, and other emotional challenges.

One of the key benefits of visualization is its ability to promote relaxation and reduce stress. When you visualize calming scenes or positive outcomes, your brain releases neurotransmitters like serotonin and dopamine, which enhance your mood and create a sense of serenity. This practice can also improve your focus and concentration, which can help you to stay present and grounded. Another significant benefit is emotional regulation. By regularly practicing this, you can train your brain to respond to stressors with calmness and clarity, rather than panic or anxiety. This makes it a valuable tool for managing emotional triggers and building resilience to them.

To get started with visualization, you can try a few simple exercises. The first is the safe place visualization. Begin by finding a quiet, comfortable space where you won't be disturbed. Close your eyes and take a few deep breaths to center yourself. Imagine a place where you feel completely safe and at ease. This could be a real location, like a favorite beach or forest, or an imaginary one. If you've seen the film *Fight Club*, you might remember that the safe place for the main character, played by Edward Norton, is an igloo, filled with penguins. Focus on the details: the sounds, smells, and sights that make this place comforting. Spend a few minutes immersing yourself in this scene, allowing the feelings of safety and peace to wash over you.

Another effective exercise in a similar vein is future self-visualization. This technique involves imagining yourself in the future, having achieved your goals and overcome your challenges. Visualize yourself as confident, happy, and fulfilled. What does this future self look like? How do they feel? What advice would they give you? This exercise can be incredibly motivating, helping you to connect with your potential and stay focused on your path to healing. This visualization is especially effective for those who find it difficult to image themselves in certain future situations: such as getting married, or having the job of their dreams.

The healing light visualization is a powerful method for addressing specific emotional wounds. Start by sitting comfortably and closing your eyes. Imagine a warm, glowing light above your head. This light symbolizes healing and love. As you breathe in, visualize this light entering your body, filling you with warmth and comfort. Focus on areas where you feel pain or tension, directing the light to these spots. Imagine the light dissolving any negative emotions or discomfort, replacing them with feelings of peace and healing. This technique is fantastic for bridging the gap between the physical and the mental. Often, with practice at this technique, when you are naturally exposed to light on future occasions, you can be filled with intense joy.

Incorporating such forms of visualization into your daily life requires consistency and practice. Set a regular time each day for your visualization exercises. This could be in the morning to start your day with positivity or in the evening to unwind and relax. Using guided visualization scripts or recordings can also be helpful – many of which can be found online or through various apps; audio recordings can guide you through the process step-by-step taking the pressure off at the start of this journey. With their tools and notifications it can help you remember and therefore be more constant with your meditation routine.

Let talk about Jenny; a woman who struggled with severe anxiety. By incorporating visualization into her daily routine, she found a way to manage her anxiety effectively. Each morning, Jenny practiced the safe place visualization, which helped her start the day with a sense of calm. Over time, she noticed a significant reduction in her anxiety levels and an improvement in her overall mental health. Another inspiring case is that of Mark, who used the future self-visualization to overcome his feelings of hopelessness. By regularly visualizing a positive future, Mark was able to stay motivated and focused on his goals, leading to significant improvements in his emotional well-being.

Visualization is a versatile and accessible tool that can significantly enhance your emotional healing process. By creating positive mental imagery and engaging your senses, you can reduce stress, improve emotional regulation, and build resilience. Whether you choose to visualize a safe place, your future self, or a healing light, the key is to practice consistently and make it a regular part of your routine.

3.3 CREATING A SAFE SPACE FOR YOUR INNER CHILD

Let's dig deeper into one crucial aspect – the safe space for the inner child. This space acts as a sanctuary where your inner child can express emotions freely and feel secure. A safe space is more than just a physical location; it's a mental environment that allows for a sense of emotional safety and security. Psychologically, having a safe space is crucial because it allows you to confront and process painful memories without feeling overwhelmed. When you feel safe, your brain shifts from a state of high alert to one of calm and openness, enabling deeper emotional healing.

To create a physical safe space, start by choosing a location in your home where you feel most at ease. This could be a corner of your bedroom, a cozy nook in your living room, or even a small area in your garden. The key is to select a spot where you can relax and feel at peace. Once you have chosen the location, add comforting items that evoke a sense of safety and warmth. Soft blankets, plush pillows, and gentle lighting can create a soothing atmosphere. Consider incorporating personal touches like photographs, mementos, or objects that carry positive memories. These elements can make the space feel uniquely yours, a kind of one off in the world.

Along with the physical, we must also take into account the mental safe space. This involves using visualization techniques to imagine a place where you feel completely safe and protected. Begin by sitting comfortably and closing your eyes. Take a few deep breaths to center yourself. Now, visualize a place that brings you a sense of peace. This could be a serene beach, a lush forest, or a cozy room. Focus on the sensory details of this place: the sound of the waves, the scent of pine trees, or the warmth of a fireplace. Imagine yourself fully immersed in this environment, feeling the safety and tranquility it offers. This mental visualization can provide immediate comfort and serve as a refuge during moments of emotional distress. People often call this their 'happy place', but as you see it can be mental as well as physical.

Using your safe space regularly can significantly enhance your healing process. Integrate this space into your meditation practices. Before you begin meditating, spend a few moments in your physical or mental safe space to ground yourself. After all, we as humans have a deep connection to the spaces around us; sometimes these even go unnoticed, but trust your body to intuit when a place feels good to be in. This grounding can help you enter a state of relaxation more easily and make your meditation sessions more effective. During moments of emotional distress, retreat to your safe space to find solace. Whether it's taking a few minutes to sit in your comforting corner or closing your eyes and visualizing your mental sanctuary, this practice can help you manage stress and regain emotional balance.

Incorporating your safe space into daily routines can also reinforce its benefits. You might start your day by spending a few minutes in your safe space, setting positive intentions for the day ahead – imbibing the vibe that it offers you as something unique to you. Similarly, before going to bed, use this space to unwind and reflect on the day, releasing any accumulated stress. Over time, your safe space will become an integral part of your healing, providing a constant source of comfort and security.

By establishing both physical and mental safe spaces, you create a foundation for emotional resilience and a series of overall positive projections on life. This sanctuary becomes a place of refuge, allowing you to nurture your inner child and foster deeper healing. As you continue to use and expand this space, you'll find it easier to navigate the complexities of your emotions, ultimately leading to a more balanced and fulfilling life. Take your time to get familiar with the space. In the same way we develop feelings for people, we need time to adjust and feel at ease with our safe place, but it's something worth committing time to.

3.4 ART THERAPY FOR HEALING

Art therapy is a unique and powerful way to express emotions that might be difficult to verbalize. It involves using creative processes to explore feelings, reduce stress, and gain insights into your emotional world. The primary purpose of art therapy is to provide an alternative outlet for expression, especially when words fall short. By engaging in artistic activities, you can tap into a deeper, often subconscious level of your psyche. This can reveal hidden emotions and facilitate emotional release. The benefits of art therapy are well-documented. It helps improve emotional expression, reduces stress, and enhances overall mental well-being. Moreover, it is a kind of wonderful distraction, away from a world which can at times seem mundane. With a paint pallet, or drawing pencils, you essentially have a whole new world to create at your fingertips. And, trust me on this one; you don't have to be very good! It's not really about talent; it's just about embracing the task.

One of the simplest and most effective art therapy exercises is drawing your emotions. I know what you're thinking, "How do you go about drawing your emotions?" Well, yes, it takes a little bit of creativity but it is within everyone's grasp. You'll find that it allows you to visually represent your feelings, which can be particularly helpful if you find it challenging to articulate them. Start by gathering some basic art supplies like paper, colored pencils, or markers. Sit in a quiet space and take a few deep breaths to center yourself. Think about a specific emotion you're experiencing and begin to draw what that emotion looks like to you. There are no rules or expectations here; the goal is to let your feelings flow onto the paper. You might find that certain colors or shapes naturally represent your emotions. For example, anger might be depicted with bold, jagged lines and dark colors, while sadness might appear as soft, flowing lines in muted tones. The film *Inside Out* is all about representing emotions like sadness, anger and happiness visually. I wonder if you're representations would be at all similar?

Another engaging exercise is creating a collage of positive memories. This activity not only helps you focus on the positive aspects of your life but also allows you to reconnect with happy memories. Gather magazines, photographs, and other materials that you can cut and paste. Find a large piece of paper or a poster board to serve as your canvas. Begin by selecting images and words that evoke positive feelings and memories. Arrange them on your canvas in a way that feels right to you, and then glue them down – kind of like what people do to make a scrapbook. As you create your collage, take time to reflect on each memory and the joy it brings. This exercise can be a wonderful way to lift your spirits and remind yourself of the good times in your life.

Painting a safe place for your inner child is another powerful art therapy exercise. This involves creating a visual representation of a place where your inner child feels safe and loved. Start by imagining a place that feels comforting and secure to you. This could be a real place, like a childhood home or a favorite vacation spot, or an imaginary one. Use paints or any other materials to help you bring this place to life. Don't be scared to add a dash of color. Focus on the details that make this space special and safe. As you paint, allow yourself to feel the safety and comfort that this place provides. This exercise not only helps you connect with your inner child but also reinforces the sense of safety and security that is what the process of healing is all about.

When it comes to materials and tools for art therapy, you don't need anything fancy or expensive. Basic art supplies like paper, markers, and paints are more than sufficient. You can find these items at any craft store or even use what you have at home. Optional materials like magazines for collage, clay for sculpting, or even fabric scraps can add variety to your creative flow. The key is to use materials that you feel comfortable with and that inspire you to create. Remember, the goal of art therapy is not to produce a masterpiece but to explore and express your emotions in a way that feels authentic to you. That being said, you might feel like pinning it to the fridge and being proud of it; why not?

Reflection is a crucial part of the art therapy process. After completing an art exercise, take some time to reflect on what your artwork reveals about your emotions and your inner child. Ask yourself questions like, "What feelings does this piece evoke?" or "What do the colors and shapes represent to me?" Journaling about the art-making process and its emotional impact can provide further insights and help you process your feelings. Write about your thoughts and emotions as you created the artwork, and consider how it relates to your current emotional state. This reflection not only deepens your understanding of your emotions but also reinforces the healing process.

Art therapy is a versatile and accessible tool that can significantly aid in your emotional healing. By engaging in creative activities like drawing, collage, and painting, you can express and explore your emotions in a safe and therapeutic way. The materials are easy to find, and the exercises are suitable for all skill levels. Reflecting too can provide valuable insights into your emotional world and help you connect with your inner child. Through this process, you can release pent-up emotions, reduce stress, and gain a deeper understanding of yourself. I guarantee you'll find it wonderfully cathartic, but also just a hell-of-a-lot of fun.

4

REWIRING NEGATIVE THOUGHT PATTERNS

One morning, I made a small mistake at work—nothing major, but it hit me harder than it should have. Before I knew it, I was spiraling into a pit of self-doubt. That tiny slip-up quickly grew into something much bigger in my mind. I started imagining the worst: I was convinced this one mistake would ruin my career, that I'd be seen as incompetent, and that everything I'd worked for was slipping through my fingers. The feeling of impending doom was so overwhelming that I couldn't focus on anything else.

Later that day, I met up with a close friend and, during our conversation and me telling him exactly how I was feeling, it suddenly hit me—I was catastrophizing. I had blown the situation way out of proportion, letting one minor error snowball into a full-blown crisis in my head. It was a powerful wake-up call. At that moment, I realized how deeply trapped I'd become in my own negative thought patterns. It was eye-opening, even a little frightening, to see how much power those thoughts had over me. But that moment also marked the start of something new—my journey to better understand, and hopefully rewire, these patterns that had been holding me back for so long.

4.1 IDENTIFYING NEGATIVE THOUGHT PATTERNS

Cognitive distortions are biased, irrational thoughts and beliefs that can distort your perception of reality and lead to psychological damage – so, let's work out exactly how we can recognize these awful thought tangents. Put simply, these distortions affect the way you think, feel, and behave, often without you even realizing it. They are like mental filters that twist your perception of events, making you see things in a more negative light than they actually are. They are the brain's way of simplifying complex information but often at the cost of accuracy and emotional well-being.

One common example is all-or-nothing thinking, where you see things in black-and-white terms. For instance, if you make a single mistake, you might view yourself as a complete failure, ignoring all the good things you've done. Another example is overgeneralization, where you draw broad conclusions from a single incident. If you have one bad experience, you might believe that everything will always go wrong. These thought patterns can have a significant impact on your mental health, leading to anxiety, depression, and low self-esteem. They create a cycle of negative thinking that can be hard to break. But why do we do it? Isn't it like untying your laces right before the race begins?

To identify these negative thought patterns, we need self-monitoring techniques. One effective method is keeping thought records. This involves writing down the negative thoughts you experience throughout the day, along with the situations that triggered them and the feelings they evoked. This practice helps you become more aware of your thought patterns and provides insights into how they affect your emotions and behaviors. Another useful tool is a daily thought journal. In this journal, you can record your thoughts, emotions, and reactions to different situations. Reflective questioning is also beneficial. Ask yourself questions like, "What evidence do I have for this thought?" or "Is this thought based on facts or assumptions?" These questions encourage you to critically evaluate your thoughts and challenge their validity. It's like the same kind of reasoning as when we propose such thoughts to another; somehow vocalizing these thoughts shows them in a new light which can make them seem, at best, illogical, and, at worst, frightening.

Recognizing triggers that lead to negative thought patterns is another important step. Stressful situations at work, for example, can often trigger negative thoughts. If you have a high-stress job, you might find yourself thinking, "I'll never be able to handle this," or "I'm not good enough for this role." Interpersonal conflicts are another common trigger. Disagreements with friends or family members can lead to thoughts like, "They don't care about me," or "I'm always the problem." Memories of past trauma can also trigger negative thought patterns. If you've experienced childhood trauma, certain situations or reminders can evoke thoughts like, "I'm unsafe," or "I can't trust anyone."

Consider the story of Sam, who struggled with all-or-nothing thinking. Whenever Sam faced a setback, he would immediately conclude that he was a failure. This pattern affected his self-esteem and many of his close relationships, as he often felt unworthy and tended to isolate himself away from others. Through self-monitoring and reflective questioning, Sam began to recognize this distortion. He started challenging his thoughts by asking, "Is it true that I'm a complete failure because of one mistake?" This process helped him see the broader picture and acknowledge his successes, breaking the cycle.

Emily, who frequently engaged in overgeneralization, is another wonderful example. After a difficult breakup, she convinced herself that she would never find love again. This belief led to feelings of hopelessness and prevented her from pursuing new relationships. By keeping a daily thought journal, Emily identified this pattern and began to question its validity. She wrote down instances where she had positive interactions with others and reminded herself that one bad experience didn't define her or her future. This shift in perspective helped her open herself up to new possibilities and regain hope.

Identifying negative thought patterns is a critical step in breaking their hold on your life. By understanding cognitive distortions, using self-monitoring techniques, and recognizing triggers, you can gain greater awareness of your thoughts and begin to challenge and reframe them. It's often difficult to imagine not thinking a certain way, like thinking is as fixed as the intake of air our bodies need, but we really can. Trust me; you can just as easily put a positive spin as a negative spin.

4.2 COGNITIVE BEHAVIORAL TECHNIQUES (CBT) FOR POSITIVE THINKING

We've spoken about CBT a little bit already. Let's talk about it further and think about how it may be useful in terms of reframing negativity. To begin with, at its core, CBT is based on the idea that our thoughts, feelings, and behaviors are interconnected. By changing the way we think, we can alter our emotional responses and behaviors. It focuses on identifying and challenging irrational or harmful thoughts, replacing them with more balanced and constructive ones. This approach is highly effective because it empowers individuals to take an active role in their healing process and can be done so it is personalized to the individual.

CBT works by helping you become aware of your automatic thoughts, which are the spontaneous, often negative thoughts that arise in response to specific situations. These automatic thoughts are more often than not influenced by underlying core beliefs and cognitive distortions. Once you identify these thoughts, CBT techniques guide you in challenging and reframing them, leading to healthier emotional responses and behaviors. One example of an automatic thought could be, "I'll never be good enough." What working with CBT can do is help you to examine this belief, gather evidence for and against it, and develop a more balanced perspective, such as, "I have strengths and areas for improvement, just like everyone else."

One of the most effective CBT techniques for challenging negative thoughts is Socratic questioning. This involves asking yourself a series of probing questions to examine the validity of your thoughts. For example, if you think, "I'm a failure because I made a mistake," you might ask, "What evidence do I have that supports this thought?" and "What evidence do I have that contradicts it?" This process helps you see that one mistake does not define your worth. After a time, this process can seem almost automatic, as you respond *ad hoc* to situations. Another technique is gathering evidence for and against your thoughts. This involves writing down facts that support or refute your negative thoughts, providing a clearer, more balanced view. Reframing negative thoughts into positive ones also forms part of the process. If you catch yourself thinking, "I can't handle this," try rephrasing it to, "This is challenging, but I have the skills to manage it." It can be a little tough at first to lean towards the positive side, but the questioning can help you reach that point.

Like many of the techniques in this book, practice makes perfect. Start by writing down your negative thoughts and then actively creating positive alternatives. This might feel forced at first, but with repetition, it becomes more natural. For example, if you often think, "I'm not good at anything," replace it with, "I have many skills, and I'm constantly learning and growing." Practicing new thought patterns daily helps reinforce these positive alternatives. You can set aside a few minutes each day to review your alternative thoughts and repeat them to yourself. Over time, this practice helps rewire your brain, making positive thinking essentially on auto-pilot. It's a wonderful and seamless moment that you can reach in your progression towards improved self-esteem.

CBT, as a global practice, offers various practical tools and worksheets to support this process. Templates to record your thoughts or "Thought Record" templates are one such tool. These guide you in documenting your automatic judgments, the situations that triggered them, and the emotions they evoked. By reviewing these records, you can identify patterns and work on challenging and reframing your thoughts. Cognitive restructuring worksheets are another valuable resource. These worksheets help you deconstruct negative thoughts and rebuild them in a more balanced and accurate way. For instance, a cognitive restructuring worksheet might include sections for identifying a negative thought, gathering evidence for and against it, and developing a balanced alternative. Think of yourself as a prosecutor, gathering evidence.

To illustrate the benefits, consider the example of a completed CBT worksheet. Imagine you had the thought, "I'm terrible at my job because I missed a deadline." The worksheet guides you to write down this thought, list the emotions it triggered (e.g., anxiety, shame), and then gather evidence. You might note that you have received positive feedback from your boss in the past and that missing one deadline doesn't invalidate your overall performance. Finally, you develop a balanced thought, such as, "Missing a deadline doesn't define my abilities. I can learn from this and improve my time management skills." What we aim to do, through this process, is build resilience, so we are ready to take on other invasive thoughts further down the line.

To sum up, CBT offers a structured, effective approach to transforming negative thought patterns. By challenging and reframing harmful thoughts, developing healthier alternatives, and using practical tools like worksheets, you can cultivate a more positive, balanced mindset. Think of it as rewriting the story of your experience – set yourself up as a new character in this narrative, one who is sure to take on the world with a newness and positivity that you felt little of before beginning this process.

4.3 DAILY AFFIRMATIONS TO COUNTERACT NEGATIVE THOUGHTS

An affirmation is a positive statement or phrase that is often repeated with the intention of reinforcing a belief. Let's think about how we can use these to best effect. To create personalized affirmations, start by identifying the negative thoughts you frequently struggle with. If you're a person who often thinks, "I'm not good enough," you can craft an affirmation like, "I am worthy and capable." Personalization is key because generic affirmations might not resonate as deeply. Use positive, present-tense language to make your affirmations more effective. Be done with saying simply, "I will be confident," say, "I am confident." This phrasing helps your brain accept the affirmation as a current reality, making it more impactful. Focus on areas where you experience frequent negativity, such as self-worth, relationships, or work performance. Tailoring affirmations to these areas ensures they address your specific needs and challenges.

As you get ready in the morning, why not look in the mirror and repeat your affirmations out loud? This can set a positive tone for the day and boost your confidence. In the evening, take a few minutes before bed to reflect on your day and repeat your affirmations. This helps reinforce positive thoughts and encourages a restful sleep. Using affirmation apps or reminders can also be helpful. Set up notifications on your phone to remind you to say your personal phrases throughout the day. Speaking them aloud during daily activities, like driving or walking, can further ingrain them into your subconscious.

Let's take a look at some examples to help you craft your own. For a greater sense of confidence at work, you might use, "I am capable and competent in my work." This affirmation reinforces your skills and abilities. If you struggle with self-worth, try, "I deserve love and respect." This statement affirms your inherent value and reminds you that you are worthy of positive relationships. For resilience, an affirmation like, "I am resilient and can handle life's challenges," can be empowering and motivate you to think differently in the future. It acknowledges your strength and capacity to overcome obstacles. Another useful affirmation is, "I am growing and improving every day." This reinforces a growth mindset, something we've already mentioned is incredibly important, and reminds you that progress is ongoing, that life is kind of always an incomplete circle in one way or another. Tailor these examples to fit your unique experiences and needs, making them more meaningful and effective.

We've already seen the importance of journaling as a tool for deep reflection. It can be further utilized here in fact. By writing down your affirmations in your journal you reflect on how you change over time through using them, but also you can reflect on how your affirmations change, say, over a 6-month period. It's likely after all that, as you progress, your scope will change and you will include new and exciting positive statements. As you journal, ask yourself questions like, "How have my thoughts and emotions changed since I started using affirmations?" or "What positive changes have I noticed in my behavior?" Regular self-assessment helps you see the tangible benefits of affirmations and keeps you motivated to continue using them.

Let's look at a number of examples which show the effectiveness of positive affirmations. Sarah, who struggled with feelings of inadequacy at work, offers a great example. She crafted personalized affirmations like, "I am skilled and valuable in my job," and integrated them into her daily routine. Each morning, she repeated her affirmations while getting ready, and in the evening, she reflected on her achievements. Over time, Sarah noticed a significant boost in her confidence and performance at work. Journaling helped her track this progress, reinforcing the positive impact of her affirmations. She's quoted as having said, "It wasn't as hard as I'd thought it would be to maintain the routine. I just find phrases that really connect with me, and, for that reason, they just flew off the tongue".

Daily affirmations are a powerful tool; use them freely, creatively and delve into this new world of possible positivity. Let's summarize what we've discussed below:

- **Craft personalized affirmations:** Tailor your affirmations to align with your goals, values, and areas of growth. Get creative!
- **Incorporate affirmations into your routine:** Recite them during daily activities like morning rituals, exercise, or meditation. Get into a rhythm!
- **Track your progress:** Keep a journal or note changes in your mindset and behavior as a result of using affirmations. Get jotting down!

- **Overcome negativity:** Use this tool to challenge and replace self-doubt or limiting beliefs with positive thoughts. Gain a wider perspective of yourself and embrace the new you!

4.4 MINDFULNESS PRACTICES TO STAY PRESENT

We've touched upon mindfulness and its benefits. Let's look specifically now at how it can be used to stay present – i.e. to ground ourselves in the present moment. Rooted in ancient meditation traditions, mindfulness has gained significant attention in modern psychology for its benefits in mental and emotional well-being. The core principles of mindfulness include paying attention to the here and now, accepting your experiences without trying to change them, and observing your thoughts and feelings without getting caught up in them. By staying present, you can reduce the grip of negative thought patterns and create a more balanced and grounded state of mind. We might even call it objectivity.

Let's be clear: mindfulness reduces stress and anxiety – it's a fact. Numerous studies have shown clearly the benefits. But, even without these, it's clearly been helping people for centuries, if not millennia, when we think of how it is used in the Buddhist faith. When you focus on the present moment, you break the cycle of ruminating on past mistakes or worrying about future uncertainties. This shift in focus can lead to a calmer, more centered mental state; it's as if you are not being attacked from both sides, but can suddenly take a breather and gain perspective. Mindfulness also enhances emotional regulation, helping you respond to situations with greater clarity and not jump at people's throats say, or react harshly or rashly to something. It's about observing your thoughts and feelings without judgment, allowing you to gain a deeper understanding of your emotional landscape to reach that level of mental stability you desire for yourself.

Mindfulness meditation techniques offer practical ways to cultivate this present-moment awareness. Meditation that uses a body scan is a great starting point for beginners. This practice involves mentally scanning your body from head to toe, paying attention to any sensations you notice. Find a quiet place to sit or lie down, close your eyes, and take a few deep breaths. Starting from the top of your head, slowly move your attention down through your body, noting any areas of tension or discomfort. For me, I prefer to start with the temples, and breathe in and out, slightly clenching that part of the body; I then shift my focus to the skin around my eyes, then down to my mouth. I spend a lot of time around my neck as for me this is often a place with a lot of built-up tension. And I basically continue like this until I reach the toes.

Another effective technique is breath awareness meditation. This involves focusing on your breath as it flows in and out of your body (this can of course be combine with the body scan). Sit comfortably, close your eyes, and bring your attention to your breathing. Notice the sensation of the breath entering and leaving your nostrils or the rise and fall of your chest, or even your stomach as you inhale deeper and try and reach those areas further down. When your mind wanders, gently bring your focus back to your breath. This simple practice can be incredibly grounding and helps train your mind to stay present. No need to start with an hour, but you should perhaps set yourself a target; if you start with just 2-3 minutes, maybe within a few weeks, you can look to do around 10-12 minutes.

Mindfulness doesn't just involve sitting in silence with your legs crossed; there is actually quite a broad spectrum in term of how it can be used. Mindful eating is one such example. Instead of rushing through meals, take the time to savor each bite. Pay attention to the flavors, textures, and aromas of your food. This practice not only enhances the eating experience but also helps you stay present. Mindful walking is another such practice. As you walk, focus on the sensation of your feet touching the ground, the movement of your legs, and the rhythm of your breath. This can turn a simple walk into a grounding and meditative experience. Mindful listening involves giving your full attention to the sounds around you or the person speaking to you. This can in fact benefit your connection with others as you feel better prepared and have more patience when engaging in conversations.

It can also be used to interrupt negative thoughts. When you notice a negative thought arising, label it without judgment. For example, if you find yourself thinking, "I'm not good enough," simply note, "There's a thought about not being good enough." This labeling helps create a sense of distance between you and the thought, reducing its emotional impact. Bringing your focus back to the present moment is another effective strategy. If your mind starts to spiral into negative thinking, gently redirect your attention to your breath or the sensations in your body. This practice helps break the cycle of rumination and anchors you in the present. This is also a factor in how you learn to accept those negative thoughts – to see them simply as things passing over your head that you cannot reach, but that at the same time cannot really impact you. Instead of trying to suppress or fight your thoughts, acknowledge them and then let them pass, like clouds drifting across the sky. It's all about putting negative thinking in its place – giving it a new role in your life, not as advisor, but as visitor.

Mindfulness practices offer practical and effective ways to stay present, reduce negative thought patterns, and enhance overall well-being. By incorporating techniques like body scan meditation, breath awareness, and loving-kindness meditation into your daily life, you can cultivate a more mindful and balanced approach to life. These practices not only help you manage stress and anxiety but also foster deeper self-awareness and emotional resilience. As you continue to explore mindfulness, you'll find that it becomes a valuable tool for navigating life's challenges with greater clarity and compassion.

5

EMOTIONAL REGULATION TECHNIQUES

One afternoon, I was deep in conversation with a close friend and what had started as a casual chat slowly morphed into something all the more tense, and before I even noticed the shift, my chest began to tighten. My heart started pounding in that way it does when you feel cornered, misunderstood, or even attacked. In that moment, I could feel myself becoming defensive – lowering the drawbridge - a surge of anger building up, as if every part of me was ready to snap.

But later that evening, after the dust had settled, it hit me: I hadn't just been angry, I'd been triggered. That surge of emotion wasn't just about the argument we'd had—it was rooted in something deeper, something buried that had been stirred up. Emotional triggers are like that. They strike when you're least prepared, blindsiding you with reactions that feel so automatic, so overwhelming.

It's in moments like these that you realize the importance of really understanding yourself. Taking the time to notice these triggers, and learning how to manage them, is a vital step toward emotional well-being. Because once you see them for what they are, they stop controlling you—and that's when you begin to heal, to grow, and to respond, rather than react.

5.1 UNDERSTANDING EMOTIONAL TRIGGERS

Emotional triggers are stimuli that provoke intense emotional reactions, often rooted in past experiences. These triggers can be anything from specific words and situations to certain people or places. They act as reminders of past traumas, causing your body and mind to react as though the original event is happening all over again. Triggers are deeply personal and can vary widely from person to person. For example, a simple comment about your appearance might trigger feelings of insecurity if you were often criticized as a child. These emotional reactions are not always rational, but they are often powerful and can significantly impact how well you feel after they arise.

As we mentioned, the development of emotional triggers is closely linked to past experiences and traumas. When you experience something traumatic, your brain encodes the associated emotions and physical sensations. This response is driven by the amygdala, the part of your brain responsible for processing fear and emotional reactions, which triggers a heightened state of alertness whenever similar situations arise. Later in life, similar stimuli can evoke these same reactions, even if the current situation is not threatening. In such a way, someone who experienced bullying at school might feel a surge of fear and defensiveness in any situation that resembles their past experiences. Common triggers include rejection, betrayal, unjust treatment, and feeling excluded or disapproved of. These triggers can manifest in various ways, such as a pounding heart, sweaty palms, or a sense of dread. For me personally, it's often a need to escape – to get out of the place ASAP!

Identifying your personal emotional triggers should be the first step toward managing them. One effective method is to keep a trigger journal. Document situations that provoke strong emotional reactions, noting the specific trigger and your response, then, over time, you'll see that patterns emerge, helping you understand what sets off your emotional reactions. Reflecting on past emotional reactions can also provide insights. Think back to times when you felt overwhelmed by your emotions. What was happening at the time? What were you thinking and feeling? Recognizing physical signs of being triggered is equally important. Pay attention to changes in your body, such as increased heart rate, muscle tension, or shallow breathing (feeling like you cannot get enough air). These physical cues can alert you to the presence of a trigger before your emotions spiral out of control.

The impact of emotional triggers on behavior and relationships can be profound. Consider the case of Alex, who reacts intensely whenever his partner raises their voice. Alex's father was verbally abusive, and loud voices trigger a fight-or-flight response in him. This reaction has caused numerous conflicts in his relationship, as his partner feels unfairly attacked and misunderstood. Another example is Jessica, who becomes withdrawn and distant whenever she feels criticized at work. Her past experiences of harsh criticism have left her hypersensitive to feedback, affecting her performance and relationships with colleagues. Both cases here illustrate the emotional impact that past traumas can have on your lived experience in the present.

Managing emotional triggers requires a proactive approach. One such way is through a trigger action plan. Start by identifying your common triggers and the situations in which they occur. Then, outline specific steps you can take to manage your reactions. For example, if you know that certain conversations with a family member trigger you, plan to take a break or use a calming technique when you feel the trigger arising. Practicing self-soothing techniques is another effective strategy. Techniques such as deep breathing, progressive muscle relaxation, or visualization can help calm your nervous system and reduce the intensity of your emotional reactions. Seeking support from trusted individuals is also crucial. Talk to friends, family members, or a therapist about your triggers and how they affect you. Having a support system can provide validation and practical advice for managing your emotions.

So, through identifying your triggers, recognizing their impact, and implementing strategies to manage them, you can reduce the power they hold over you. This proactive approach empowers you to navigate your emotions with greater awareness of how they have been impacting you and it will help you to learn that they are not the be-all and end-all.

5.2 MINDFULNESS-BASED STRESS REDUCTION

Mindfulness-Based Stress Reduction (also known as MBSR) is a therapeutic technique that focuses on bringing your attention to the present moment. It was developed by Jon Kabat-Zinn in the 1970s at the University of Massachusetts. The primary goal of MBSR is to help you experience thoughts and feelings non-judgmentally, which can significantly reduce stress and improve emotional regulation. By practicing mindfulness, you learn to observe your thoughts and feelings without getting caught up in them, allowing you to respond to stressors more calmly and effectively.

One of the key benefits of MBSR is its effectiveness in managing stress. When you practice mindfulness, you engage the parasympathetic nervous system, which helps counteract the body's stress response. This can lead to a reduction in cortisol levels, the hormone associated with stress. Additionally, MBSR promotes emotional regulation by helping you stay present and grounded, reducing the intensity of negative emotions. Studies have shown that MBSR can alleviate symptoms of anxiety, depression, and chronic pain, making it a versatile tool for improving overall well-being.

The basic principles of MBSR revolve around being present in the moment, practicing non-judgmental awareness, and accepting your current experiences. Being present means focusing your attention on the here and now, rather than dwelling on the past or worrying about the future, or having your mind jump from thought to thought in what often feels like an uncontrolled manner. This shift in focus helps you break the cycle of rumination and so reduces stress because you are effectively reducing the load. Non-judgmental awareness involves observing your thoughts and feelings without labeling them as good or bad. This practice generates a sense of curiosity and openness, allowing you to explore your inner world without self-criticism. Acceptance means acknowledging your current experiences, even if they are uncomfortable, without trying to change them.

Several MBSR techniques can help integrate mindfulness into your everyday life. Of course, you can do those we've already mentioned such as body scan meditation, breathing exercises or loving-kindness meditation, but here are some further options. One foundational practice is sound meditation. This involves sitting comfortably in a quiet space and focusing on the sounds around you, both near and far. Instead of seeking out specific sounds, let your awareness expand to notice the subtle noises you might usually ignore—like the hum of a fan or distant traffic. The goal is to observe these sounds without labeling them or getting attached, simply allowing them to come and go. This practice cultivates a sense of present-moment awareness and helps ground you in your environment.

Mindful stretching is another useful component of MBSR. Engage in gentle stretches, paying attention to how your muscles feel as you move. You can incorporate basic movements like reaching your arms overhead, bending forward, or twisting gently from side to side. Focus on the sensations in your body as you stretch— notice areas of tightness, tension, or relaxation. Moving slowly and mindfully can help release physical tension and foster a greater connection with your body. For me personally, although guided yoga and stretching videos are great, I just love to take my time over things, go at my own speed and really dig deep into stretches, feeling every inch of the body, and focusing on the tight areas which I can then work on at my own pace.

Integrating MBSR into your daily life requires regular practice and commitment. Set aside time each day to try some of the techniques mentioned above, even if it's just a few minutes. Consistency is key to reaping the benefits of MBSR. Make sure to incorporate it into daily activities, such as eating, walking, or even brushing your teeth. Focus on the sensations, smells, and tastes, and engage fully in the experience. Using mindfulness to manage stress at work can also be beneficial. Take short breaks throughout the day to practice mindful breathing or a quick body scan. This can help you stay calm and focused, improving your productivity and reducing stress.

5.3 BREATHING EXERCISES FOR EMOTIONAL CALM

Breathing is a fundamental yet often overlooked aspect of emotional regulation. When you face stress or anxiety, your body's natural response is to prepare for "fight or flight," causing rapid, shallow breathing. This response, while useful in genuine danger, can exacerbate feelings of anxiety and stress in everyday situations. Controlled breathing can counteract this response by activating the parasympathetic nervous system, something we've highlighted already above but which is so vital here. The result: a simple reduction in stress. The act of deep breathing basically sends signals to your brain to tell it that it's okay to relax, reducing the production of stress hormones like cortisol and promoting a sense of calm.

One of the simplest and most effective breathing techniques is diaphragmatic breathing, also known as belly breathing. To practice this, find a comfortable position, either sitting or lying down. Place one hand on your chest and the other on your belly. Inhale deeply through your nose, allowing your belly to rise while keeping your chest relatively still. Exhale slowly through your nose or mouth, feeling your belly fall. Repeat this process for several minutes, focusing on the rise and fall of your belly. This technique helps you take fuller breaths, increasing oxygen intake and promoting relaxation. You may find that you can breathe in to the count of 11 or even 12 seconds. It's obviously not a competition, but try to see how slow and controlled you can breathe into that lower part of your body.

Box breathing is another useful technique, especially for those moments when you need to quickly regain composure. Imagine drawing a box with your breath. Inhale through your nose to a count of four, hold your breath for another count of four, exhale through your mouth for four, and then hold again for four. Repeat this cycle several times. This method not only helps calm the mind but also improves focus and concentration. The structured nature of this technique makes it particularly effective for situations where you need to quickly reduce stress and regain control.

The 4-7-8 breathing technique, popularized by Dr. Andrew Weil, is excellent for promoting relaxation and for when you want to decompress before going to bed. To practice this, sit or lie down comfortably. Inhale quietly through your nose to the count of four. Hold your breath to the count of seven. Exhale completely through your mouth, making a whoosh sound, to the count of eight. Repeat the cycle three to four times. The making of the sound here can feel really nice, as if your body is producing something via breathing; it also stimulates your auditory senses as you listen in to the sounds you're producing.

Alternate nostril breathing, or Nadi Shodhana, is a traditional yogic practice that balances the mind and body. Sit comfortably up straight. Use your right thumb to close your right nostril and inhale deeply through your left nostril. Close your left nostril with your right ring finger, release your right nostril, and exhale through it. Inhale through the right nostril, then close it and exhale through the left. Continue this alternating pattern for several minutes. This technique not only calms the mind but also balances the flow of energy in the body, promoting overall well-being.

Using these breathing exercises in real-time during stressful situations can be incredibly effective. Before a big presentation, take a few minutes to practice diaphragmatic breathing or 4-7-8 breathing. This can help calm your nerves and improve focus. During moments of conflict, such as an argument with a partner or colleague, use box breathing to regain composure and prevent reactive responses. These techniques can be your go-to tools for managing stress and maintaining emotional balance in challenging situations.

Creating a daily breathing practice can significantly enhance your ability to manage stress and maintain emotional calm. Set aside a specific time each day for focused breathing exercises. This could be in the morning to start your day with a sense of calm or in the evening to unwind before bed. Combine breathing exercises with other relaxation techniques, such as meditation or progressive muscle relaxation, for added benefits. Using breathing apps or guided recordings can also help you stay consistent and provide additional guidance. Apps like Calm or Headspace offer guided breathing sessions that can be easily integrated into your daily routine. Or, alternatively, do what feels good; listen carefully to your body and react accordingly.

5.4 GROUNDING TECHNIQUES FOR EMOTIONAL STABILITY

Grounding techniques are practical methods designed to anchor you in the present moment, providing a sense of stability and calm. They work by refocusing your attention away from distressing thoughts and emotions and onto the physical world around you. The primary purpose of grounding is to manage anxiety and emotional overwhelming situations, which can often arise from past traumas presenting themselves in present stressful situations. Grounding helps you regain control over your emotional state by creating a mental and physical distance from the triggers that cause distress.

Let's focus first on the benefits for reducing anxiety. When you feel overwhelmed, grounding techniques can help you connect with your immediate surroundings and bring your focus back to the present moment. This shift in attention can alleviate the intensity of the emotional reaction and provide a sense of relief.

Physical grounding techniques are straightforward and can be easily incorporated. The 5-4-3-2-1 sensory technique is a simple yet effective method to regain your center. Start by identifying five things you can see, four things you can touch, three things you can hear, two things you can smell, and one thing you can taste. This exercise engages all your senses, helping you become more aware of your surroundings and less focused on your distressing thoughts. Another practical technique is grounding through physical touch. Holding an object, such as a smooth stone or a stress ball, can provide a tactile sensation that retain that grip on the world through touch. Focus on the texture, weight, and temperature of the object, allowing these sensations to anchor you in the present moment. Movement-based grounding, such as walking or stretching, can also be beneficial. Pay attention to the sensation of your feet hitting the ground or the stretch of your muscles. This physical activity helps release tension and provides a sense of connection to your body.

Mental grounding techniques are equally valuable for staying present and focused. Close your eyes and imagine a place where you feel completely safe and at peace. This could be a real location, like a beach or a forest, or an imaginary one. Focus on the details of this place—the sounds, smells, and sights. This mental image can provide a sense of comfort and security, and can help you manage emotional distress. Reciting affirmations or mantras is another effective technique. Choose a phrase that resonates with you, such as "I am safe" or "This too shall pass." Repeat this phrase silently or aloud, focusing on the words and their soothing effect. Mental exercises, like counting backward from 100 or listing categories (e.g., types of animals or favorite foods), can also help divert your mind from distressing thoughts and bring your attention back to the present moment.

Incorporating grounding techniques into your daily routine can strengthen emotional stability and help you manage stress more effectively. When feeling overwhelmed, use grounding to quickly regain control. For example, if stress arises at work, pause for a few minutes to practice the 5-4-3-2-1 sensory method or focus on a grounding object to redirect your attention.

Make grounding part of your morning routine to start the day with calm and clarity. Begin with a brief visualization of your safe place or repeat a calming affirmation. Combining grounding techniques with other practices, like mindfulness or breathing exercises, can amplify their benefits. For instance, try mindful breathing while holding a grounding object or incorporate grounding during meditation for a deeper sense of presence.

As you explore these techniques, remember that finding what works best for you may take some trial and error. Stay patient and compassionate with yourself throughout this process. In the next chapter, we will delve into building trust and healthy relationships, essential for nurture deeper connections and emotional growth.

6

BUILDING TRUST AND HEALTHY RELATIONSHIPS

I often sit in cafes and people watch. Maybe you do the same? Once, I was watching people interact around me and I noticed the ease with which friends laughed together and couples shared moments of intimacy. It's a beautiful thing. It struck me how trust seemed to be the invisible thread weaving these connections; the cornerstone of any healthy relationship. Yet, for many of us, it is a fragile and elusive quality, especially if we've experienced trauma. Whether stemming from childhood neglect, betrayal in relation-ships, or things which align with our cultural memories within our family or even as an entire nation, trauma can severely erode our ability to trust. Rebuilding this trust is not just about mending relationships with others but also about learning to trust ourselves again.

6.1 REBUILDING TRUST AFTER TRAUMA

Let's focus a little on just what is at stake when trust is missing from the formula due to the surfacing of past events. Trauma, particularly from childhood or toxic relationships, can create deep-seated trust issues. When you've been betrayed or abandoned by those you depended on, it's natural to develop a guarded, skeptical outlook on life. This erosion of trust is a protective mechanism, shielding you from further harm. However, it also isolates you, making genuine connections difficult. Fear plays a significant role in cutting short the trust we have at our disposal. The fear of being hurt again can be so overwhelming that it prevents you from opening up to others. This fear often manifests as hypervigilance, constantly scanning for signs of betrayal or disappointment, which can strain even the healthiest of relationships. Remember, it's much easier to find something that you've actually been searching for. Trauma also impacts self-trust. When those who were supposed to protect and nurture you let you down, it can lead to self-doubt and confusion. You might question your own judgment, making it hard to trust your decisions and instincts. What remains important is to release ourselves from this constant spiral of negativity.

Rebuilding trust in oneself is the foundation for trusting others. Start with self-validation exercises. These exercises involve acknowledging and affirming your thoughts and feelings. For example, when you feel anxious or doubtful, tell yourself, "It's okay to feel this way; my feelings are valid." This practice helps you reconnect with your inner self and builds a sense of self-worth. Again, writing down your thoughts here can be an incredibly proactive approach. Why not jot down your accomplishments and positive qualities. Write about times when you overcame challenges or made good decisions. Reflecting on these moments can boost your confidence and remind you that you are capable. Over time, these practices can help you rebuild the trust you once had in yourself.

Building trust with others should be a gradual process. Start with low-stakes trust-building activities. Engage in situations where the risk of betrayal is minimal but the potential for positive reinforcement is high. As an example, share a small personal story with a friend and observe their reaction. Notice if they listen attentively and respond with empathy. These small acts of trust can gradually build a foundation for deeper connections. Trust is not built overnight though; it requires patience and ongoing assessment. Pay attention to how people in your life behave consistently. Are they reliable? Do they keep their promises? Consistent positive behavior reinforces trust and helps you feel more secure in your relationships. Let others know that you are working on rebuilding trust and that it might take time. Honest conversations about your fears and expectations can strengthen understanding and patience from those around you.

Real-life examples can offer hope and practical insights. Consider the story of Rachel, who had trust issues due to a toxic relationship in the past. When she met her new partner, she was upfront about her struggles with trust. Her partner responded with patience and understanding, consistently showing reliability and empathy. Over time, Rachel's trust grew, and she found herself opening up more, leading to a healthy and fulfilling relationship. Another example is David, who had a strained relationship with his father due to childhood neglect. As an adult, David decided to rebuild this relationship. He started with small interactions, like casual conversations and shared activities. By observing his father's consistent efforts to connect and support him, David gradually rebuilt trust, leading to a stronger and more meaningful bond.

Trust issues stemming from trauma can be deeply ingrained, but they are not impossible to overcome. By taking actionable steps to rebuild trust in yourself and others, you can create healthier, more fulfilling relationships. Remember, the journey to rebuild trust is gradual and requires patience and persistence. With time and effort, you can overcome the barriers that trauma has placed on your ability to trust.

6.2 COMMUNICATION SKILLS FOR HEALTHY RELATIONSHIPS

When I think back to some of the most challenging moments in my relationships, poor communication often played a starring role. Effective communication is the lifeblood of any healthy relationship. It's the bridge that connects us, allowing us to share our thoughts, feelings, and needs. When communication breaks down, misunderstandings and conflicts arise, leading to emotional distance and resentment. In most partnerships, communication acts as a gauge, reflecting the health and stability of the connection between you both. However, several barriers can hinder effective communication, such as assumptions, distractions, and emotional triggers. These barriers create an environment that leads to misinterpretations and conflicts, undermining trust and intimacy in relationships.

Why not give active listening a go? It involves fully engaging with the speaker, showing that you value and understand their perspective. Start by maintaining eye contact, which signals attentiveness and respect. When your partner speaks, focus on their words and body language, resisting the urge to interrupt. Reflecting back on what the other person says is something that few of us do, but can be incredibly eye-opening. This involves paraphrasing their statements to confirm your understanding. For example, if your friend says, "I've been feeling really stressed at work," you might respond, "It sounds like work has been overwhelming for you lately." This not only shows that you are listening, but also that you are validating their feelings. Asking clarifying questions can further enhance understanding. Instead of making assumptions, ask open-ended questions like, "Can you tell me more about what's been stressing you out?" This invites deeper conversation and fosters a sense of connection.

Expressing your needs and boundaries clearly is vital for maintaining healthy relationships. Using "I" statements can help you express your feelings and needs assertively without sounding accusatory. For instance, instead of saying, "You never listen to me," try, "I feel unheard when I don't get a chance to share my thoughts." This shifts the focus from blaming the other person to expressing your own experience. Setting boundaries without guilt is equally important. Boundaries are about self-respect and communicating what is acceptable to you. Role-playing scenarios can be a helpful practice. For example, if you need to set a boundary with a colleague who frequently interrupts you, you might practice saying, "I appreciate your input, but I need to finish my point before we move on." This rehearsal can build your confidence and make it easier to assert your boundaries in real situations.

Conflict is inevitable in any relationship, but how you handle it determines exactly what the result may turn out to be. One effective conflict resolution skill is staying calm during disagreements. When emotions run high, it's easy to say things you don't mean. Take a few deep breaths or a short break if needed to regain your composure. Finding common ground and compromising is another key strategy. Instead of focusing on winning the argument, aim to understand the other person's perspective and find a solution that satisfies both parties. Apologizing and forgiving effectively are also crucial. A sincere apology acknowledges the impact of your actions on the other person. For example, "I'm sorry for raising my voice earlier; I didn't mean to hurt you."

Forgiveness, on the other hand, involves letting go of resentment and moving forward with a blank canvas.

Consider the story of Mia and Jake, a couple who struggled with communication in their early years together. Mia often felt that Jake didn't listen to her, leading to frequent arguments. After learning about active listening, Jake made a conscious effort to maintain eye contact, reflect back Mia's words, and ask clarifying questions. This small change had a profound impact on their relationship, making Mia feel heard and valued. They also practiced expressing their needs using "I" statements, which reduced misunderstandings and strengthened their bond.

In another case, Sarah had a difficult time setting boundaries with her family. She felt overwhelmed by their constant demands but was afraid of hurting their feelings. Through role-playing scenarios and using "I" statements, Sarah learned to assert her boundaries respectfully. She communicated her need for personal time by saying, "I love spending time with you, but I need some alone time to recharge." Her family respected her boundaries, leading to healthier and more balanced relationships.

Good communication is essential for building strong, healthy relationships. By truly listening to others, being clear about what you need, and setting boundaries, you create a space for deeper connections. Plus, developing skills to resolve conflicts can help you tackle challenges with ease. These abilities not only strengthen your relationships but also give you the confidence to express yourself authentically.

6.3 SETTING AND MAINTAINING HEALTHY BOUNDARIES

Boundaries are the invisible lines that define what is acceptable and unacceptable in our interactions with others. They are essential for emotional health and healthy relationships because they protect your well-being and ensure that your needs are met. Physical boundaries refer to your personal space and physical touch. Emotional boundaries involve separating your feelings from the emotions of others and knowing where your emotional needs end and theirs begin. Without clear boundaries, you might find yourself feeling resentful, exhausted, or overwhelmed. Poor boundaries can lead to codependency, where you prioritize others' needs over your own, or enmeshment, where you feel responsible for others' emotions and well-being. Recognizing when boundaries have been set inadequately is something we should all consider. If you often feel taken advantage of or struggle to say no, it may be time to reevaluate your boundaries.

Identifying personal boundaries begins with self-reflection. Start by writing about situations where you felt uncomfortable or violated. What happened, and how did it make you feel? Reflecting on these experiences can help you identify your limits. Consider prompts like, "When have I felt overwhelmed by others' demands?" or "What behaviors leave me feeling respected?" Another exercise is to list your values and priorities. Understanding what is important to you can clarify where your boundaries need to be set. Reflect on past experiences when perhaps there was an overstepping of the boundaries you'd wanted. Have there been times when you successfully set boundaries? What made it work? Conversely, think about times when you got your wires crossed concerning the limits that needed to be in place. What could have been done differently?

Communicating your expectations in terms of boundaries is key to maintaining them. Use assertive language that is clear, but at the same time respectful. Instead of saying, "You never listen to me," try, "I need to feel heard when we talk." This approach focuses on your needs without blaming the other person. Setting boundaries in different contexts requires tailored strategies. For example, at work, you might say, "I am unable to take on additional tasks right now as I am focusing on current projects." With family, you might set boundaries by saying, "I need some quiet time each evening to recharge." In friendships, you could express a boundary by saying, "I value our time together, but I need to limit our outings to once a week." Having scripts for common boundary-setting situations can make these conversations easier. Why not practice a little before you say them to the other party?

Maintaining boundaries consistently is just as important as setting them. Regularly reassess your boundaries to ensure they still align with your needs and values. Circumstances in life often change, and so might your boundaries. Be open to adjusting them as you see fit. Handling boundary violations requires a firm yet respectful approach. If someone crosses a boundary, address it promptly. You might say, "I felt uncomfortable when you did that. Please respect my boundaries in the future." Try to be consistent with it too. If you allow violations to go unchecked, it sends a message that your boundaries are not important and you may leave the door open to them being overstepped in the future. Self-care practices support boundary maintenance. Prioritize activities that nurture your well-being, such as exercise, hobbies, or spending time in nature. Practicing self-compassion is also vital. Remind yourself that setting and maintaining boundaries is a form of self-respect and self-care.

Consider the story of Emily, who struggled with setting boundaries with her overbearing mother. Emily felt drained and resentful but feared hurting her mother's feelings. After reflecting on her needs, Emily decided to set clear boundaries. She communicated her need for personal space by saying, "Mom, I love spending time with you, but I need some evenings to myself to relax." Her mother initially resisted, but Emily remained consistent and respectful. Over time, her mother learned to respect her boundaries, seeing that it had been placing an unnecessary toll on her daughter, leading to a healthier and more balanced relationship.

Another example is Alex, who had some difficulties work. He often took on extra tasks, leading to him feeling completely burnt-out. By reflecting on his limits, Alex learned to say no to additional responsibilities. He communicated this to his boss by saying, "I appreciate the opportunity, but I need to focus on my current projects to ensure quality work." His boss respected his decision, and Alex found a better work-life balance.

Boundaries are the foundation of healthy relationships. They protect your emotional health and ensure that your needs are met. By identifying, communicating, and maintaining boundaries, you can create more balanced and fulfilling interactions. Remember, setting boundaries is an act of self-respect and self-care, essential for feeling good and getting on with others.

6.4 CULTIVATING VULNERABILITY

Vulnerability is the cornerstone of deep, meaningful connections. It involves opening up and sharing your true self with others, including your fears, hopes, and insecurities. This kind of openness can be scary, especially if past experiences have taught you to keep your guard up. It's important to realize that being vulnerable is not the same as oversharing. It means sharing your inner world in a way that invites connection and understanding, while oversharing can overwhelm others and may stem from a need for validation rather than genuine connection. The benefits of being vulnerable in relationships are immense. To start with, it allows for a deepened sense of trust, promotes intimacy, and creates a space where both parties feel safe to be their authentic selves. When you allow yourself to be vulnerable, you signal to others that you trust them, which encourages them to do the same in turn. This mutual openness can transform relationships, making them stronger and more resilient.

Let's look at how to go about producing spaces for this new-found vulnerability. Start by choosing the right people. Not everyone is equipped to handle your deepest fears and insecurities. Look for individuals who have shown empathy, understanding, and respect in your interactions in the past. These are the people who are more likely to respond positively to your displays of this challenging position. Establishing mutual trust and respect is also essential. This involves being reliable, keeping confidences, and showing genuine interest in each other's well-being. When both parties feel respected and valued, it creates the conditions to explore vulnerability better. Setting up a physical environment that feels safe can further encourage openness. This might be a cozy corner of your home, a quiet café, or a peaceful spot in nature. The goal is to create a space where you feel comfortable and at ease, which makes it easier to open up.

In this safe space, start by sharing minor personal details. This could be something like a childhood memory or a favorite hobby. Observe how the other person responds. Are they attentive and empathetic? Positive reactions to these small disclosures can build your confidence to open up further. Gradually, open up about deeper emotions as you feel more comfortable. You don't have to reveal everything at once. Take your time and allow the relationship to develop naturally. Reflecting on the experience of being vulnerable can provide valuable insights. After you've shared something personal, take a moment to consider how it felt. Did you feel relief, fear, or something else? Understanding your emotional response can help you navigate future instances of vulnerability.

Handling reactions to your vulnerability is an important skill. Not everyone will respond positively, and that's okay. Coping with rejection or misunderstanding can be challenging, but it's crucial to remember that these reactions are not a reflection of your worth. If someone responds negatively, take a step back and evaluate the situation. Are they going through their own struggles? Might that have influenced their reaction? Use this as a learning experience to better understand yourself and others. Celebrating positive responses is equally important. When someone responds with empathy and understanding, acknowledge and appreciate it. Learning from each experience of being vulnerable can help you grow. Each instance, whether positive or negative, being this way offers insights into your own emotional landscape and the dynamics of your relationships.

Consider the story of Anna, who had always struggled with vulnerability due to a childhood marked by emotional neglect. She decided to start small by sharing a minor personal detail with her friend Lisa. Lisa responded with genuine interest and kindness, which encouraged Anna to open up more. Over time, Anna found herself sharing deeper emotions and experiences, leading to a stronger and more supportive friendship. On the other hand, when Anna shared her feelings with a colleague who responded dismissively, she learned to be more discerning about whom to trust with her vulnerabilities. Each experience taught her valuable lessons about herself and her relationships.

Vulnerability is a powerful tool for building deep, meaningful connections. By creating safe spaces, practicing vulnerability gradually, and learning to handle various reactions, you can amplify both the trust and intimacy in your relationships. Remember, being vulnerable is a sign of strength, not of weakness. It takes courage to open up, but the rewards are well worth it.

As we move forward, let's look at how some of the patterns of anxiety and fear show themselves intergenerationally.

ROCKETMAN AND INNER CHILD
HEALING

"When we honor our inner child's feelings, we release the emotional hurts that we're still subconsciously carrying around."

— PATRICIA HOPE

I want to pause for a moment now to give you a movie recommendation—yes, really! If you haven't seen it before, I'd highly recommend looking up *Rocketman*. It's a biopic of Elton John, whose early trauma had a profound effect on his life, leading him to addiction and a constant yearning to be loved. The movie follows his journey as he tries to balance his life in the limelight with his needs as a human being. I won't give the story away, but what I will say is that there comes a point where Elton realizes that he can be happy without the approval of his parents or a partner and that the key to happiness is for him to love and accept himself. There's a moment where he hugs a younger version of himself, which represents a massive turning point for him in his journey in coming to terms with his past. Essentially, the adult and child parts of himself reintegrate in this moment, showing that Elton is embracing the small, scared part of himself and giving him the love he always deserved. I think this movie has a lot to say about inner child healing and how powerful it is in us learning to love and accept ourselves, no matter how much this was lacking in our childhood.

We've all been through different experiences, and since most of us aren't rock stars, our lives probably don't look a lot like Elton's. Yet we all have an inner child who still carries various levels of trauma, and reparenting that child can do a lot to heal the pain and loneliness we've carried into adulthood. There are many people who are looking for that kind of healing, and my motivation for writing this book was to make the journey easier for as many people as I can… and this is the point where I'd like to ask for your help. You can help me to reach more readers by leaving a review of this book online.

By leaving a review of this book on Amazon, you'll help other people find an accessible way into inner child healing and find the guidance they need to start soothing those old wounds.

Reviews help to connect books with the readers who are looking for them, so a few words from you could make a huge difference—just as my recommendation of *Rocketman* could motivate you to go and watch the movie (I really hope you do!)

Thank you so much for your support. This is a journey we all have to make alone, but we can help each other out along the way.

Scan the QR code below

7

BREAKING GENERATIONAL TRAUMA CYCLES

Growing up, I couldn't shake the feeling that my family's struggles were following a script written long before I was born. My grandmother would recount stories from her youth—tales of loss, poverty, and resilience, like worn pages in a book she knew by heart. I'd hear echoes of those same struggles in my parents' lives and, eventually, in my own. At first, I dismissed it all as coincidence, but as I dug deeper into the idea of generational trauma, I realized these weren't just random misfortunes. They were patterns—silent legacies etched into our lives, repeating themselves over and over. It was a chilling thought, as if the past had slipped into our present like an unwelcome guest. But recognizing it gave me a strange sense of power. I began to see a way out —a path to healing and rewriting the stories that had bound us to certain behaviors and ideals for so long.

7.1 UNDERSTANDING GENERATIONAL TRAUMA

Generational trauma, also known as intergenerational or trans-generational trauma, refers, as the words would imply, to the transmission of trauma from one generation to the next. This cycle of trauma can stem from various sources, including abuse, discrimination, natural disasters, and war. In essence, it is the emotional and psychological residue left by traumatic experiences that then gets passed down through families over time. This passing down happens not only through genetics but also through behaviors, communication patterns, and coping mechanisms. For example, children of Holocaust survivors often exhibit signs of trauma, even if they haven't experienced the horrors firsthand. This phenomenon illustrates the deep and lasting impact that such horrific events can have.

The historical context of generational trauma is vast and varied. It is often seen in communities though that have faced significant collective trauma, such as Black Americans or Indigenous populations. These groups have endured systemic oppression, violence, and displacement, which have left lasting scars on their descendants. For instance, the trauma experienced by enslaved Africans has permeated through generations, manifesting in ongoing struggles with identity, mental health, and societal integration. Similarly, Indigenous communities continue to grapple with the effects of colonization, which has disrupted their cultural practices and inflicted widespread psychological harm.

As we mentioned in our introduction, generational trauma is transmitted through multiple mechanisms, both biological and environmental. One of the most intriguing biological mechanisms is epigenetics, which involves changes in gene expression caused by environmental factors. Trauma can leave epigenetic marks on DNA, which can be passed down to subsequent generations. These marks do not alter the DNA sequence itself but affect how genes are turned on or off. Research on Holocaust survivors and their descendants has shown alterations in the hypothalamic-pituitary-adrenal (HPA) axis, which regulates stress response. These alterations are similar to those observed in individuals with post-traumatic stress disorder (PTSD), indicating a biological link between parental trauma and offspring's mental health. Research around this topic though is in its early stages and a lot more work needs to be done to assess the real impact.

Environmental factors also play a crucial role in the transmission of generational trauma. Learned behaviors and coping mechanisms are often passed down within families. For example, a parent who experienced trauma may develop maladaptive coping strategies, such as emotional avoidance or hypervigilance. These behaviors can be modeled and adopted by their children and so forth, perpetuating a cycle of trauma. Family dynamics and communication patterns further reinforce this cycle. In families where trauma has occurred, communication may be characterized by secrecy, emotional suppression, or conflict. These learned patterns can create an environment where trauma is continuously transmitted and reinforced, or even normalized in a way.

The impact of generational trauma on mental health is profound. Individuals affected by generational trauma are at a higher risk of developing anxiety, depression, and other mental health disorders. For example, children of parents who experienced childhood abuse often exhibit symptoms of anxiety and depression, even if they themselves were not directly abused. Relationship difficulties are also common, as generational trauma can lead to issues with trust, intimacy, and emotional regulation. Individuals may struggle to form and maintain healthy relationships, perpetuating a cycle of isolation and emotional distress.

Emotional regulation challenges are another significant effect of generational trauma. Those affected may find it difficult to manage their emotions, often experiencing intense and unpredictable emotional responses. This can lead to difficulties in daily functioning and increased vulnerability to stress. For instance, someone whose parent experienced severe trauma may exhibit heightened sensitivity to stressors and have difficulty calming down after becoming upset. These emotional regulation challenges can hinder their ability to cope with life's demands and contribute to ongoing mental health struggles. Studies on the children of mothers who experienced childhood abuse, for example, have shown lower cortisol levels and altered stress responses, further supporting the idea that trauma can be biologically transmitted across generations.

One notable case study involves a family affected by multiple generations of trauma. The grandmother, a Holocaust survivor, exhibited severe PTSD symptoms, which were mirrored in her daughter, despite the daughter not experiencing the Holocaust directly. The granddaughter too, showed signs of anxiety and depression, illustrating the far-reaching impact of generational trauma. This case underscores the importance of recognizing and addressing generational trauma to break the cycle and promote healing across generations.

7.2 IDENTIFYING INHERITED EMOTIONAL PATTERNS

Recognizing emotional patterns in your family history is a crucial step in breaking the cycle of generational trauma. Begin by creating a family tree, but instead of merely noting names and dates, focus on emotional patterns and significant events. This exercise allows you to visualize how certain behaviors and emotional responses may have been passed down. For example, you might notice that anxiety and fear are recurring themes across generations. By mapping out these patterns, you can start to understand their origins and how they have influenced your own emotional landscape. This may not be an easy task to do alone, but consider opening up to family members about this and getting them to share with you their knowledge. Who knows what useful tidbits might emerge?

The stories you come across often hold clues about the emotional experiences of your ancestors. For instance, if tales of hardship and resilience are common, it might indicate a family history of enduring significant stress and trauma. Note the emotional impact of significant events, such as the loss of a family member, financial hardships, or migration. Understanding these contexts helps you see how past traumas have shaped your family's emotional responses and coping mechanisms.

Common emotional patterns that are often inherited through generations include anxiety and fear, avoidance behaviors, issues with trust and intimacy, and recurring conflicts and misunderstandings. Anxiety and fear can manifest as a heightened sense of alertness or constant worry about the future. This pattern might stem from ancestors who lived through uncertain or dangerous times. Avoidance behaviors, such as withdrawing from social interactions or avoiding conflict, can be a learned response to past traumas. If family members have historically dealt with emotional pain by shutting down or distancing themselves, you might find yourself adopting similar behaviors.

Issues with trust and intimacy are also common in families affected by generational trauma. A history of betrayal or abandonment can create a deep-seated reluctance to form close relationships. You might find it challenging to open up to others, fearing vulnerability will lead to hurt. Recurring conflicts and misunderstandings are very often another symptom. These conflicts can perpetuate feelings of anger, resentment, and frustration, making it difficult to maintain harmonious relationships. Recognizing these patterns is the first step toward breaking them and fostering healthier emotional responses.

To help you reflect on your behaviors and emotions and identify inherited patterns, consider engaging in self-reflection exercises. Start with prompts that encourage you to explore your family dynamics, such as "What emotional patterns do I see in my family?" or "How did my parents handle stress and conflict?" Reflective questions about your personal reactions and triggers can also provide valuable insights. Ask yourself, "When do I feel most anxious, and how do I react?" or "What situations trigger strong emotional responses in me?" Comparing your behaviors with those of your family members can reveal similarities that point to inherited patterns.

Upon analysis, you might notice that your tendency to avoid confrontation mirrors your father's behavior, or your mother's, or that of your great-grandfather. Recognizing this can help you understand that your response is not just a personal flaw but a learned behavior passed down through generations. Consider the story of Laura, who always felt a sense of dread when facing new challenges. Through journaling and self-reflection, she discovered that her grandmother, who had lived through the Great Depression, often spoke of the fear and uncertainty of those times. Laura realized that this inherited anxiety had shaped her own responses to stress. By understanding this connection, pinpointing the origins of this, she was able to address her anxiety more effectively and develop healthier coping mechanisms.

Another example is James, who struggled with trust issues in his relationships. He noticed a pattern of mistrust in his family, stemming from his grandfather's experiences of betrayal during the Second World War. Through therapy and self-reflection, James began to understand how these experiences had influenced his own ability to trust others. This awareness allowed him to work on building trust and intimacy in his relationships, breaking the cycle of mistrust that had plagued his family for generations. Identifying and understanding these inherited emotional patterns is a powerful step toward healing and creating a healthier emotional legacy for the future generations to come. It might be worth exploring, not only for its healing properties, but also for the insights you can gain from other family members about their take on the world.

7.3 STRATEGIES FOR BREAKING DESTRUCTIVE CYCLES

The strategies to break these cycles are similar to other areas we've mentioned previously. Remember to look for patterns of thought and make efforts to react to them. Think about including mindfulness meditation in your day, journal for self-reflection based on the findings and notions that you may have unearthed about your family, but also do regular self-check-ins with yourself. Take a few minutes each day to ask yourself how you're feeling and why. This habit helps you stay connected to your inner state and make conscious choices to break negative cycles.

Therapeutic approaches are invaluable in breaking generational trauma cycles. Family therapy is particularly effective as it addresses the dynamics and communication patterns within the family unit. It helps family members understand each other's perspectives and work together to heal. Cognitive Behavioral Therapy (CBT), as we've already mentioned, can be a wonderful way to break these cycles. Trauma-focused therapy specifically targets the effects of trauma, helping you process and integrate traumatic experiences. Techniques such as Eye Movement Desensitization and Reprocessing (EMDR) can be used to alleviate the emotional burden of trauma. Somatic experiencing is a therapeutic approach that focuses on the body's sensations to release stored trauma. This method emphasizes the connection between the mind and body, helping you to understand how trauma manifests both physically and emotionally.

Building new habits and behaviors is crucial for replacing old, destructive patterns with constructive ones. Start by developing positive coping mechanisms. Instead of reaching for unhealthy distractions when stressed, try engaging in activities that promote well-being, such as exercise, creative hobbies, or mindfulness practices. Setting personal goals for behavior change can also be transformative. Identify specific behaviors you want to change and set realistic, achievable goals. For instance, if you tend to react with anger during conflicts, set a goal to practice deep breathing or take a pause before responding. Practicing new communication techniques is another effective strategy. Learn to express your needs and boundaries clearly and assertively. It all comes down to maintaining those healthy relationships and providing support for those you love, and seeking that same support in return.

In fact, support systems and resources are essential in the healing process. Joining support groups can provide a sense of community and shared understanding. Connecting with others who have similar experiences can be incredibly validating and offer new perspectives on healing. Seeking mentorship or coaching can also be beneficial. A mentor or coach can provide guidance, support, and accountability as you work through breaking generational cycles. Utilizing online resources and communities is another valuable option. There are numerous online forums, websites, and social media groups dedicated to healing generational trauma. These platforms offer a wealth of information, support, and connection with others on a similar path.

Finally, let's look at a real example. Sarah, who struggled with anxiety and avoidance behaviors inherited from her mother, offers an insightful case. Through mindfulness meditation and regular journaling, she became more aware of her triggers and emotional responses. Engaging in trauma-focused therapy helped her process her childhood experiences, while family therapy improved her relationship with her mother. Sarah also joined an online support group, where she found a community of individuals facing similar challenges. By setting personal goals and practicing new communication techniques, Sarah gradually replaced her old patterns with healthier ones. Her journey illustrates how self-awareness, therapeutic approaches, new habits, and support systems can work together to break destructive cycles and create lasting change.

7.4 CREATING A NEW LEGACY FOR FUTURE GENERATIONS

This all begins with setting intentional family goals. These should reflect the values and aspirations you have for your family. Start by identifying core family values. These might include respect, empathy, resilience, or honesty. Discuss these with other family members to ensure everyone is on the same page. Once you have a clear understanding of your core values, set both short-term and long-term goals that align with these principles. Short-term goals might involve weekly family meetings to discuss everyone's feelings and experiences, while long-term goals could include creating a family tradition of annual retreats focused on bonding and self-improvement. A family mission statement can serve as a guiding star, encapsulating your collective vision and commitment to these goals. This statement should be a collaborative effort, reflecting the input and agreement of all family members.

Practicing healthy communication within the family is pivotal to a supportive and nurturing environment. It's important to remember here what we've already discussed about active listening – taking the time to really focus on what people are saying. For example, during a family meeting, take turns speaking and listening, ensuring each member feels heard and valued. Think also about how best to resolve conflicts which may arise. Teach your family to address disagreements calmly and constructively. Encourage everyone to express their feelings using "I" statements, such as "I feel hurt when..." instead of "You always + something negative". This approach reduces defensiveness and promotes understanding. Taking the time to organize these meetings can also be very constructive, as we perhaps allow time to celebrate our achievements and reflect on internal worries and concerns with a view to overcoming them.

Modeling positive behaviors is one of the most impactful ways to influence future generations. Children and young adults often emulate the actions and attitudes of their role models. Part of this is learning how to regulate emotions so you can be an effective role model. Show your family how to manage stress and emotions healthily, whether through deep breathing, taking a break, or discussing feelings openly. Another element involves practicing empathy and compassion. Make it a habit to consider others' perspectives and respond with kindness. Encourage your family to do the same by acknowledging and validating each other's feelings. Also, allow for an environment where the open expression of feel-ings is welcomed and encouraged. Let your family know that it's okay to share their emotions: whether it's joy, sadness, anger, or fear. This openness creates a supportive atmosphere where everyone feels safe to be themselves.

Celebrating progress and milestones is a powerful way to rein-force positive change and acknowledge growth. Create family traditions to celebrate achievements, no matter how small. This could be a monthly "family success night" where you recognize accomplishments. Everyone, every day is achieving something; it just might take a little effort from yourself or members of your family to highlight such successes. In addition to this, take a moment to look back on the goals you've set and the strides you've made – both individually or as a family unit. Discuss what's working and what might need adjustment. Creating a family scrapbook can be a wonderful way to capture and cherish milestones. Encourage each family member to contribute by adding photos, mementos, and notes about their achievements, challenges, and reflections. This scrapbook not only serves as a visual record of growth but also as a source of inspiration and cherished memories for everyone.

In setting intentional family goals, practicing healthy communication, modeling positive behaviors, and celebrating progress, you create a nurturing environment that breaks the cycle of generational trauma. These steps help build a legacy of resilience, empathy, and emotional well-being, ensuring that future generations inherit a healthier emotional landscape. Remember, the journey to creating a new legacy is ongoing, requiring patience, commitment, and a willingness to grow together. As you continue to implement these practices, you'll pave the way for a brighter, more connected future for your family.

8

FOSTERING SELF-AWARENESS AND PERSONAL GROWTH

One sunny afternoon, while tending to my garden, I found my mind wandering back to a recent conflict with a colleague. As I dug my hands into the soil, it struck me that my reaction had been far more intense than the situation called for. This sudden moment of clarity made me realize just how essential self-awareness is for personal growth. In fact, in many ways, the one reacts directly to the other. It was a simple, quiet task that sparked this insight, yet its impact was profound. Self-awareness serves as the foundation of emotional intelligence and personal development, allowing us to recognize our emotions, thoughts, and behaviors, and understand how they shape our interactions with others.

Let's begin by exactly what we mean by self-awareness, then think about ways that we can activate this skill for self-betterment. Self-awareness is the ability to see yourself clearly and objectively through reflection and introspection. It's more than just knowing your likes and dislikes; it's about understanding your emotional triggers, strengths, weaknesses, and the impact of your behavior on others. According to emotional intelligence experts, self-awareness is the first step in managing your emotions and developing better relationships. When you are self-aware, you can identify what you are feeling and why, which helps you respond to situations in a more balanced and thoughtful way. This heightened sense of awareness is crucial for both personal and professional life. It allows you to navigate challenges with greater ease, make informed decisions, and cater to healthier relationships.

Of course, mindfulness is a wonderful way to gain a better understanding of ourselves. Feel free to gloss over previous mentions in previous chapters which detail how best to incorporate mindfulness into your routine. Alongside this though is the use of mirror exercises, which are especially effective when it comes to fostering self-awareness. Stand in front of a mirror and observe your facial expressions. Notice the lines, the way your eyes move, and the expressions that come naturally. Pay attention to any physical sensations or emotional reactions that arise. This exercise can be revealing, as it helps you see yourself from an external perspective. It encourages you to observe without judgment, cultivating a sense of acceptance and understanding. Another variant of this exercise involves speaking affirmations out loud to yourself in the mirror. Notice how you react to your own words and expressions, which can provide insights into your self-perception and emotional state.

Seeking feedback from others is another valuable way to gain insights into your patterns of behavior. Ask trusted friends, family members, or colleagues for their observations about your behavior. Use open-ended questions like, "How do you perceive my reaction to stress?" or "Can you share an instance where you felt I handled a situation well?" Reflect on the feedback without becoming defensive. This can be challenging, but it's essential for growth. Use the feedback constructively to identify areas for improvement and to reinforce your strengths. Remember, the goal is not to seek validation but to gain a deeper understanding of your reactions and the way the world observes you.

To deepen your self-awareness, try maintaining a diary dedicated to tracking your emotional triggers and physical reactions. Record instances that elicit strong feelings, and make note of how your body responds—whether through tension, sweating, or an increased heart rate. This reflective practice allows you to spot patterns in your emotional landscape and gain insights into how your body reacts to various situations. Additionally, you might consider exploring coping strategies or relaxation techniques to manage these responses. Over time, this proactive approach will empower you to better recognize your triggers and respond to them with greater mindfulness and control.

Incorporating these strategies into your daily life can significantly enhance your self-awareness and lead to personal growth. Let's look at one or two activities that you might consider using to help you along on this journey:

Exercises for Self-Awareness

Body Scan Meditation

- Lie down or sit comfortably.
- Close your eyes and take a few deep breaths.
- Start from your toes and slowly move up to your head, noticing any sensations or tension.
- Observe without judgment, simply acknowledging what you feel.

Mirror Exercise

- Stand in front of a mirror and relax.
- Observe your facial expressions and note any physical sensations or emotional reactions.
- Speak affirmations to yourself and notice how you react.

Seeking Feedback

- Ask a trusted friend or family member for feedback on your behavior.
- Use open-ended questions to gain deeper insights.
- Reflect on the feedback without becoming defensive, and use it for self-improvement.

Keep a Diary

- Reflect on experiences to enhance the attention you lavish on yourself.

8.2 REFLECTIVE JOURNALING FOR PERSONAL GROWTH

We've spoken previously about the incredible benefits of journaling. If you haven't yet tried it out, here might be a great opportunity to do so. Let's look more specifically at how it can be used as a reflective practice to aid in self-discovery. Essentially, this task involves writing about your thoughts, feelings, and experiences to gain deeper insights, but in such a way that the practice becomes auto-reflective, i.e. you're promoting looking back at yourself – understanding yourself through a new lens. Although the ultimate goal is self-improvement, don't let this big objective put you off; it's about starting something that will encourage more positive behaviors going forward. Reflective journaling is not just about recording events; it's about exploring your inner world and uncovering the underlying motivations and beliefs that drive you. The act of writing itself can be therapeutic, providing a safe space to process complex emotions and gain clarity.

The benefits of reflective journaling are extensive. Most importantly, as far as I'm concerned, is that it can highlight areas where you need to change and help you set goals for personal development. Moreover, journaling can improve mental well-being by providing an outlet for stress and anxiety. Writing about your worries can help you process them and reduce their emotional impact. Additionally, journaling can enhance problem-solving skills by allowing you to analyze situations from different perspectives and come up with creative solutions. After all, the student who never even opens their math's textbook is the least likely to get the correct answer.

Daily reflection prompts can guide your journaling practice and help you explore different aspects of your life. For instance, start with questions like, "What did I learn about myself today?" This prompt encourages you to reflect on your day and identify any new insights or realizations. Another useful prompt is, "How did I handle challenges today?" This helps you analyze your responses to difficult situations and assess what worked and what didn't. "How did I react to bad news today?" is another excellent prompt. These prompts can be varied to cover different areas of your life, such as relationships, work, personal goals, and emotional well-being. By regularly using these prompts, you can gain a comprehensive understanding of yourself and your life. Keep it simple; use "How" to help produce questions to reflect on the specific way in which you reacted.

It doesn't end though with the act of writing; what you are making is a tool – one which you are sharpening constantly. Heading back and reading over your journal entries can highlight key insights and patterns that you might not notice in the moment of writing. For example, you might see recurring themes, such as certain emotions or behaviors that come up repeatedly. Noting these patterns can help you identify areas that need extra focus and would benefit from being changed. Additionally, tracking changes in your thoughts and behaviors can provide a sense of progress and accomplishment. You might notice that you handle certain situations better over time or that your emotional responses become more balanced. Keeping track of these changes can motivate you to continue your personal growth journey and reinforce positive habits.

Combining journaling with other self-awareness practices can enhance the benefits. Journaling after mindfulness meditation can deepen your insights. Meditation helps you clear your mind and connect with your inner self, making it easier to reflect on your thoughts and emotions. After meditating, take a few minutes to journal about your experience. Write about any thoughts or feelings that came up during meditation and explore their significance. This can help you gain a deeper understanding of your inner world and integrate the insights from your meditation practice into your daily life. Another way to enhance your journaling practice is to use it to complement therapy sessions. Therapy provides valuable insights and guidance, and journaling can help you process and integrate these insights. After a therapy session, write about what you discussed and reflect on how it applies to your life. This can help you internalize the lessons from therapy and make lasting changes.

8.3 IDENTIFYING YOUR CORE BELIEFS

Core beliefs are the deeply ingrained assumptions and convictions that shape how you see yourself, others, and the world. These beliefs are often formed during childhood and can significantly impact your thoughts, behaviors, and emotions. They act as filters through which you interpret experiences and make decisions. Let's look at an example. Let's say that you hold the core belief that you are unworthy, you might shy away from opportunities or relationships that could bring you happiness and fulfillment. These beliefs can be positive and empowering or negative and limiting, affecting every aspect of your life, from your self-esteem to your interactions with others.

To uncover limiting core beliefs, it's crucial to engage in honest self-reflection. Besides from the techniques already mentioned above, you could try noting down recurring negative thoughts. Whenever you find yourself thinking something negative, like "I'm not good enough" or "I always mess things up," write it down. Over time, you'll notice patterns emerging. Reflect on past experiences and their impact on these beliefs. For example, if you were constantly criticized as a child, you might have developed a belief that you're inherently flawed. Identifying patterns of self-sabotage is also essential. Notice if you tend to undermine your own efforts or create obstacles that prevent you from achieving your goals. These behaviors often stem from limiting beliefs that you may not even be aware of.

Challenging and replacing limiting beliefs involves a process called cognitive restructuring. This technique helps you question the validity of your negative beliefs and replace them with more positive and realistic ones. Start by writing down a limiting belief, then list evidence for and against it. If you believe "I am a failure," note instances where you succeeded at something. This exercise helps you see that your limiting belief is not entirely accurate. Next, create affirmations to reinforce your new beliefs. Affirmations are positive statements that counteract negative thoughts. For instance, replace "I am a failure" with "I am capable and have achieved many things." Repeating these affirmations daily can help rewire your brain to adopt these new, empowering beliefs.

Creating a belief system aligned with your personal goals involves identifying beliefs that support your aspirations and values. Start by defining what you want to achieve and the values that are important to you. Then, develop beliefs that align with these goals. For example, if you want to advance in your career, adopt the belief "I am capable of achieving my goals." If happiness and well-being are important to you, believe "I deserve happiness and success." To foster a growth mindset, embrace the belief "I can learn and grow from every experience." These empowering beliefs provide a strong foundation for personal growth and help you navigate life's challenges with confidence and resilience.

By understanding and reshaping your core beliefs, you can transform how you perceive yourself and the world around you. This process requires patience and persistence, but the rewards are there to be reaped. As you replace limiting beliefs with empowering ones, you'll notice a positive shift in your thoughts, behaviors, and overall well-being. This transformation not only enhances your personal growth but also empowers you to achieve your goals and live a more fulfilling life.

8.4 TECHNIQUES FOR PERSONAL EMPOWERMENT

Personal empowerment is about taking control of your life and making decisions that align with your values and goals. It's the process of gaining confidence in your abilities and taking proactive steps to shape your future. It's deeply connected to self-efficacy, which is the belief in your ability to succeed. When you feel this way, you have a sense of control over your circumstances and are more likely to take action towards your goals. This confidence translates into better mental health, improved relationships, and greater overall satisfaction in life. Feeling empowered means believing in your potential and taking responsibility for your growth and happiness.

Setting and achieving personal goals is the main component of personal empowerment. The SMART framework is an effective method for setting goals that are Specific, Measurable, Achievable, Relevant, and Time-bound. Start by identifying your short-term and long-term goals. Short-term goals might include daily or weekly tasks, while long-term goals could span months or even years. Breaking goals into actionable steps helps make them more manageable. For example, if your long-term goal is to run a marathon, your short-term steps might include daily runs, increasing your distance each week, and joining a local running group for support. Tracking progress is vital for maintaining motivation. Celebrate milestones, no matter how small, to keep yourself motivated and acknowledge your hard work.

Building self-efficacy involves developing a strong belief in your capabilities. One effective strategy is visualizing success. Take a few moments each day to imagine yourself achieving your goals. Picture the steps you'll take, the obstacles you'll overcome, and how you'll feel once you've succeeded. This mental practice can boost your confidence and prepare your mind for success. Try to find time to reflect on things that have already made you the individual you are today. Make a list of your achievements, big and small. Remind yourself of the challenges you've faced and how you overcame them. This can provide a sense of pride and reinforce your belief in your abilities. Seeking out and accepting challenges is also crucial. Step out of your comfort zone and take on tasks that push your limits. Whether it's learning a new skill, taking on a leadership role, or tackling a difficult project, embracing challenges helps you grow and build resilience.

So, how do you feel about cultivating a growth mindset? Are you ready to take to heart that your abilities and intelligence can be developed through effort and learning? Are you ready to embrace challenges as an opportunity for growth? Remember, instead of avoiding difficult tasks, view them as chances to learn and improve. When you encounter setbacks, see them as learning experiences rather than failures. This shift in perspective can reduce fear of failure and encourage perseverance. Practicing resilience is also essential for a growth mindset. Understand that growth takes time and effort, and that setbacks are a natural part of the process. Develop strategies to cope with difficulties, such as seeking support from friends and family, practicing self-care, and maintaining a positive attitude. Over time, these practices can help you develop a growth-oriented mindset that supports personal and professional growth.

Chapter 8 has discussed the importance of self-awareness for personal growth, emphasizing its role in emotional intelligence. We've defined self-awareness as understanding one's emotions, thoughts, and behaviors, and we've highlighted mindfulness, mirror exercises, and seeking feedback as practical tools to foster it. The chapter has also explored reflective journaling as a way to gain deeper insights into who you really are and manage emotional triggers. Identifying and challenging core beliefs is crucial to personal empowerment, along with setting goals and building self-efficacy through visualization, celebrating progress, and embracing a growth mindset for continuous development.

9

INTEGRATING VARIOUS THERAPEUTIC APPROACHES

On a gray, rainy afternoon, I sat in my therapist's office, feeling overwhelmed by emotions I couldn't quite trace. Years of battling these feelings had left me drained and uncertain. My therapist gently introduced me to Cognitive Behavioral Therapy (CBT), explaining how it could help untangle the complicated web of thoughts and behaviors that had followed me since childhood. That moment marked the beginning of a profound journey—one that would lead me to healing, self-discovery and a newfound emotional resilience. It was the first step toward understanding the roots of my inner child and reclaiming control over my life. Alongside CBT, let's also focus in this chapter on a wider range of approaches: Jungian Archetypes, Regression Therapy and the best way to integrate and/or combine these approaches together.

9.1 THE ROLE OF CBT IN INNER CHILD HEALING

We've touched on CBT in previous sections already but let's dig deeper into the theory behind it in order to better put it to effective use. In the context of inner child healing, CBT is particularly effective because it addresses the maladaptive behaviors and cognitive distortions that often arise from unresolved childhood trauma. By targeting these negative patterns, CBT helps reframe past experiences, fostering a healthier self-image and emotional resilience.

CBT is built on several key principles. First, it emphasizes the importance of recognizing and challenging negative thoughts. These thoughts often stem from deep-seated core beliefs formed during childhood. For example, if you grew up feeling unloved or unworthy, you might carry these beliefs into adulthood, affecting your self-esteem and relationships. CBT helps you identify these core beliefs, examine their validity, and replace them with more positive and realistic ones. This process, known as cognitive restructuring, is central to CBT. It involves breaking down complex problems into manageable parts, allowing you to see them more clearly and address them effectively.

If you didn't already try the recommendation from earlier on to put CBT into practice, you can take a moment now to try this method involving the reframing of thoughts. Start by writing down a negative thought you often have, such as "I am not good enough." Next, ask yourself questions to challenge this belief: "What evidence do I have that supports this thought? What evidence contradicts it?" This process helps you see the thought from a different perspective, making it easier to replace it with a more balanced view, like "I have strengths and weaknesses, just like everyone else." What we ultimately looking for by doing this is a more realistic sense of the sense, one that is constructive, rather than built through fantastical thoughts or delusions.

Another powerful CBT technique is maintaining thought records. These records help track your emotional responses to various situations, making it easier to identify patterns and triggers. Start by noting the situation that triggered the emotional response, followed by the automatic thought that came to mind. Then, document your emotional and physical reactions. Finally, challenge the thought by asking questions and writing down a more balanced perspective. For example, if you felt anxious about a presentation at work, your thought record might look like this: **Situation:** Preparing for a presentation at work. **Automatic Thought:** "I will mess up and everyone will think I'm incompetent." **Emotional Response:** Anxiety, fear. **Physical Response:** Sweaty palms, racing heart. **Challenging Questions:** "Have I successfully given presentations before? What evidence do I have that I will mess up?" **Balanced Thought:** "I have prepared well and have done this successfully in the past."

Exposure exercises are also a crucial component of CBT, particularly for confronting fears related to past traumas. These exercises involve gradually exposing yourself to the feared situation in a controlled and safe manner, helping you build tolerance and reduce anxiety over time. For instance, if you have a fear of abandonment stemming from childhood, you might start by imagining scenarios where you feel alone, gradually working up to situations where you face the fear in real life. The goal is to desensitize yourself to the fear, making it less overwhelming and more manageable.

Consider the case of Julia, who struggled with a deep-seated fear of abandonment due to her parents' divorce when she was young. Through CBT, Julia began by identifying her core belief that she was unlovable and destined to be abandoned. She kept thought records to track her emotional responses during moments of anxiety, such as when her partner was late coming home. By challenging her automatic thoughts and engaging in exposure exercises, Julia gradually dismantled her fear. She started by visualizing scenarios where she reassured herself of her worth, eventually practicing self-compassion during instances of real-life anxiety. Over time, Julia developed a healthier self-image and a more secure attachment to her partner.

Similarly, consider Michael, who dealt with childhood anxiety stemming from being bullied at school. His core belief was that he was weak and incapable of defending himself. Through CBT, Michael kept detailed thought records, identifying patterns in his anxiety and challenging his automatic thoughts. He engaged in exposure exercises, starting with imagining confrontational scenarios and gradually practicing assertiveness in real-life situations. Michael's confidence grew, and his anxiety diminished, illustrating the transformative power of CBT. None of these happen overnight, but the quicker you start, the quicker you'll see results.

Remember to integrate CBT with other elements we've discussed previously: mindfulness, journaling, and self-compassion practices. Through this, you create a comprehensive and effective healing approach. This integration not only addresses the cognitive aspects of your trauma but also nurtures your emotional and psychological well-being, paving the way for lasting change and growth.

9.2 JUNGIAN THEORY AND ARCHETYPES

During a particularly introspective phase of my healing process, I stumbled upon the works of Carl Jung. His theories on the collective unconscious and archetypes resonated deeply, providing a new lens through which to understand my inner world. Jung introduced the concept of the collective unconscious, a part of the unconscious mind shared by all humans, containing archetypes—universal symbols and themes that recur across cultures and time.

These archetypes, according to Jung, are inherited potentials which shape our experiences and responses. They are deeply embedded in our psyche, influencing our behaviors, dreams, and even our healing processes.

Archetypes are the recurring symbols or motifs in our psyches that represent universal patterns of human nature. Jung identified several key archetypes, each with distinct characteristics and influences on our behaviors and emotions. The relevance of these archetypes to understanding the workings of the inner child is profound. They help us understand the different facets of our personalities and how our childhood experiences have shaped them. By engaging with these archetypes, we can gain insights into our unconscious motivations and start the healing process.

One of the most significant archetypes in Jungian theory is the Child. This archetype represents innocence, potential, and new beginnings. It embodies the wonder and curiosity of childhood, as well as the vulnerability and need for protection. When working with the inner child, connecting with this archetype can help us reclaim our sense of wonder and creativity while addressing feelings of vulnerability and insecurity. It reminds us of the untapped potential within us and the importance of nurturing our inner selves.

Another crucial archetype is the Shadow. This represents the repressed aspects of ourselves that we often deny or hide. It includes our fears, insecurities, and darker impulses. Confronting the Shadow is essential for inner child healing because it allows us to acknowledge and integrate these hidden parts of ourselves. By bringing the Shadow into the light, we can better understand our reactions and behaviors, leading to greater self-acceptance and emotional balance.

The Hero archetype symbolizes the part of us that strives to over-come challenges and achieve greatness. It embodies courage, determination, and resilience. Engaging with this archetype can be incredibly empowering for inner child work. It helps us recognize our strengths and the resilience we've developed through our struggles. By connecting with them, we can find the courage to face our past traumas and move forward with confidence.

The Caregiver archetype represents nurturing and protection. It embodies the qualities of compassion, empathy, and selflessness. When working with the inner child, connecting with this persona can help us develop a more nurturing relationship with ourselves. It encourages us to practice self-compassion and provide the care and support our inner child needs to heal.

Exploring these archetypes can be done through various tech-niques. Guided imagery is a powerful method for connecting with each of the archetypes. Begin by finding a quiet space and closing your eyes. Take a few deep breaths to relax. Visualize the arche-type you wish to connect with, such as the Child or the Hero. Imagine this figure standing before you. Take note of its appear-ance, energy, and the feelings it evokes. Engage in a dialogue with this archetype, asking questions and listening to their responses. It may be challenging to access this persona, but the more you prac-tice, the easier it gets. Often, it's the same way in which we build a character for a story; we give them a personality, an identity and an image. Through doing this we can better realize their function, and resonate with them in a more profound way.

Carrying out dialogues or role-plays with different aspects of the self can also be beneficial. For example, you can write a conversa-tion between your adult self and your inner Child. Ask your inner Child how it feels and what it needs. Respond with empathy and understanding, offering reassurance and support. This dialogue can help bridge the gap between your conscious mind and unconscious emotions, facilitating healing and integration. Some people find this kind of abreaction difficult, but we do it every day without even realizing – we have conversations with others; why not with ourselves if it is for our own betterment?

Creative expression through art and writing is another effective technique for working with archetypes. You might create artwork representing the different archetypes within you, such as drawing your inner Child or painting your Hero. Writing stories or poems that explore these archetypes can also be therapeutic. These creative practices allow you to externalize and process your inner experiences, making them more tangible and accessible.

Laura struggled with feelings of inadequacy and fear of failure. Through guided imagery, she connected with her inner Hero, visualizing herself as a courageous warrior overcoming obstacles. This visualization helped her tap into her inner strength and resilience. She began to see her challenges as opportunities for growth rather than insurmountable barriers. Laura's newfound confidence and determination significantly improved her self-esteem and ability to face life's difficulties.

Similarly, James had a deep-rooted fear of rejection stemming from childhood experiences. By engaging with his Shadow archetype through dialogue exercises, he confronted his fears and insecurities. He realized that these feelings were a natural part of his psyche, not something to be ashamed of. This awareness allowed James to integrate his Shadow, leading to greater self-acceptance and emotional balance.

Working with Jungian archetypes offers a unique and powerful approach to inner child healing. These universal symbols and themes provide a framework for understanding the different facets of our personalities and the impact of our childhood experiences. Don't feel overwhelmed; I know it may seem like a very original concept to most of you reading this. Let this be just an introduction, and a stepping stone to further research you can do by yourself or with a professional who works in this area.

9.3 REGRESSION THERAPY FOR TRAUMA RECOVERY

I remember a session where my therapist guided me into a relaxed state and asked me to recall a specific childhood memory. As I closed my eyes, vivid images and emotions began to surface—feelings of being lost and scared in a crowded store, unable to find my mother. This technique, known as regression therapy, was a profound experience that allowed me to access and process deeply-buried emotions. Regression therapy is a type of psychotherapy that helps individuals access past experiences and traumas stored in the subconscious mind. It aims to bring these buried memories to the forefront, allowing for emotional release and healing.

Regression therapy employs various techniques to access and process past traumas. One common method is hypnotic regression, where a therapist uses hypnosis to guide the individual into a deeply relaxed state. In this state, the mind becomes more open to recalling suppressed memories. Another technique is age regression, where the therapist helps the individual mentally return to a specific age or event to explore and address unresolved issues. The purpose of these techniques is to uncover the root causes of current emotional and psychological challenges, providing a pathway to healing.

The benefits of regression therapy for trauma recovery are significant. By accessing and processing past traumas, individuals can release buried emotions that may manifest as physical or emotional symptoms, such as anxiety, depression, or chronic pain.

This therapeutic approach allows for the resolution of unresolved issues, leading to a greater sense of emotional freedom and well-being. Additionally, regression therapy can help individuals gain insights into their behaviors and thought patterns, fostering self-awareness and personal growth.

For those interested in exploring regression therapy, guided techniques can be incredibly effective. Begin finding your quiet place or your safe place in your home. Once you feel relaxed, imagine traveling back in time to a specific age or event that you want to explore. Allow any images, sensations, or emotions to come to the surface without judgment. If you encounter a painful memory, practice self-compassion and reassure your inner child that you are there to provide comfort and support.

Visualization is also a powerful tool. As you revisit past experiences, visualize yourself as an observer, watching the events unfold without becoming overwhelmed. This perspective allows you to process the emotions and gain insights without reliving the trauma. Techniques for reparenting the inner child during regression are essential here as you build on working through and fixing past traumas. Imagine yourself as a nurturing adult providing the love, protection, and validation your inner child needed at that time. Speak to your inner child with kindness and reassurance, offering words of comfort and understanding. Not sure where to start exactly – visualizing a hug may be the best option at the outset.

Consider the story of Sam, who struggled with chronic anxiety stemming from childhood neglect. Through guided regression therapy, Sam accessed memories of being left alone for long periods, feeling scared and unloved. By revisiting these memories and providing comfort to his inner child, Sam was able to release the buried emotions and understand the root of his anxiety. This process significantly improved Sam's emotional well-being and reduced his anxiety.

Another example is Rachel, who experienced severe self-doubt and low self-esteem due to childhood bullying. During regression therapy, Rachel revisited the painful memories of being teased and ostracized by her peers. By using visualization techniques and reparenting her inner child, Rachel provided the validation and support she lacked during those years. This experience allowed her to heal the deep wounds of her past, leading to a more positive self-image and greater self-confidence.

9.4 COMBINING THERAPY TECHNIQUES FOR HOLISTIC HEALING

Combining various therapeutic approaches can create a comprehensive and effective healing experience. Each method offers unique strengths, and integrating them allows for a more holistic approach that addresses multiple facets of trauma. For instance, Cognitive Behavioral Therapy (CBT) can effectively change negative thought patterns, while mindfulness practices enhance present-moment awareness. When used together, these methods not only reframe harmful beliefs but also foster a sense of calm and emotional balance. Addressing different aspects of trauma ensures that you are not just treating symptoms but also tackling the root causes, leading to more sustainable healing and overall well-being.

Developing a personalized healing plan involves several key steps. Start by identifying the main areas you need to focus on—whether it's managing anxiety, improving self-esteem, or healing past traumas. Once you've pinpointed these areas, select appropriate therapeutic methods that align with your needs. For example, if you struggle with persistent negative thoughts, CBT may be beneficial.

If you have difficulty staying present, mindfulness techniques could be helpful. Create a structured yet flexible plan that incorporates these methods. Begin with a daily schedule that includes time for meditation, journaling, and CBT exercises. Flexibility is crucial; adjust your plan as you discover what works best for you. A professional should be able to assist you with a plan if you're finding it difficult to get a structure that works for you.

There are numerous ways to integrate different therapeutic techniques into a cohesive healing practice. One effective approach is to combine CBT with mindfulness and self-compassion. Start your day with a mindfulness meditation to center yourself, followed by a CBT exercise to challenge any negative thoughts that arise. Throughout the day, practice self-compassion by gently reminding yourself that it's okay to make mistakes and that you deserve kindness. Another example is using art therapy alongside regression techniques. After a regression session, where you revisit and process past traumas, engage in art therapy to express and externalize the emotions that surfaced. Drawing or painting your feelings can make them more tangible and easier to understand.

Again, journaling can also be seamlessly integrated with guided visualizations. Begin by writing about your current emotional state and any challenges you're facing. Then, engage in a guided visualization to explore these issues more deeply. Imagine a safe place where you can confront your fears or a future self who has overcome current struggles. Afterward, journal about the insights and emotions that emerged during the visualization. This practice not only deepens your self-awareness but also reinforces the positive changes you're working towards.

Tracking your progress and adjusting your healing plan is essential for sustained growth. Keep a healing journal where you document your daily practices, insights, and emotional responses. This journal serves as a valuable tool for self-assessment and reflection. Regularly review your entries to identify patterns and changes in your thoughts and behaviors. Schedule self-assessment check-ins, perhaps weekly or monthly, to evaluate your progress and adjust your techniques as needed. If you find that a particular method isn't as effective as you'd hoped, be open to trying something new. Flexibility and willingness to adapt are key to a successful healing journey.

So, to sum up, employing a combination of therapeutic techniques allows for a more comprehensive and sustainable approach to healing trauma. Integrating methods such as Cognitive Behavioral Therapy (CBT) with mindfulness, art therapy with regression techniques, or journaling alongside guided visualizations addresses various dimensions of emotional recovery, promoting overall mental well-being.

This chapter has highlighted the profound impact of combining different therapeutic modalities for holistic healing. Techniques like CBT, mindfulness, and regression therapy, when used together, help address multiple layers of trauma and support the development of a more balanced, resilient self. As you refine and adapt your personalized healing plan, maintaining flexibility and practicing self-compassion are critical to success. This integrated approach not only improves emotional health but also equips you to handle life's challenges with greater confidence and ease.

Next, let's delve into navigating and managing emotional triggers, providing practical strategies to maintain emotional stability and resilience in the face of life's inevitable challenges. This chapter will build on the techniques we've discussed, offering you further tools to create lasting change and emotional freedom.

NAVIGATING AND MANAGING EMOTIONAL TRIGGERS

I remember enjoying myself at a wedding on one occasion; the drinks were flowing, the bride and groom sauntered around the venue, chatting with all the guests. The vibe really was wonderful. From out of nowhere, just as the speeches were beginning, I felt a sudden pang of anxiety wash over me. My heart began to pound, and my palms became sweaty. What surfaced in me was a painful memory – one of rejection, in fact. I was baffled at how such a random negative thought could materialize from what was an incredibly happy occasion. For me, I used this as a springboard to understand where the thought might have come from – to understand exactly what were the feelings that led up to this. In other words, I took time later to examine and interrogate this pattern of thinking. This experience made me realize the importance of understanding and managing emotional triggers to maintain emotional stability as a way to improving my overall well-being.

10.1 RECOGNIZING YOUR EMOTIONAL TRIGGERS

Emotional triggers are stimuli that provoke intense emotional reactions, often linked to past experiences or traumas. These triggers can be specific words, situations, or even sensory reminders like smells or sounds. Essentially, they act as flashbacks, bringing painful moments from the past into the present. Understanding emotional triggers is crucial for anyone seeking emotional health and stability. They are not just about the immediate reaction but are deeply rooted in your psychological history and emotional landscape.

Triggers occur because the brain stores sensory stimuli related to traumatic events, which can later reactivate associated feelings. For instance, if you experienced severe criticism as a child, a simple comment from a coworker might trigger feelings of inadequacy and fear. Common triggers include rejection, betrayal, unjust treatment, and criticism. These triggers can vary widely from person to person, but the intensity of the emotional reaction is often out of proportion to the current situation, reflecting unresolved past experiences.

Identifying your personal triggers requires a high level of self-awareness and reflection. One effective method is keeping a log of all your triggers. This involves documenting situations that provoke strong emotional responses. Note the specifics: what happened, how you felt, and any physical reactions you experienced. Over time, patterns will emerge, helping you pinpoint what sets off these intense emotions. Reflecting on past emotional reactions can also provide valuable insights. Think back to times when you felt overwhelmed, anxious, or angry. What were the common elements in those situations? Noting physical and emotional responses is equally important. Physical symptoms like a racing heart, sweaty palms, or a tight chest can signal that you've been triggered before your mind even registers it. Heed these warning signs and use it as a learning experience.

Understanding the root causes of your emotional triggers involves delving deep into your past experiences and traumas. This process can be challenging but is essential for healing. Linking triggers to past experiences helps you see the connection between your present reactions and past traumas. For example, if you find that being ignored by a partner triggers intense feelings of abandonment, it might be linked to a childhood experience of neglect or loss. Understanding the connection between past trauma and present triggers can allow you to see that your reactions are not just random but are deeply rooted in your personal and unique history. This understanding can be the first step toward healing.

To aid in this process, several practical self-assessment tools can help you identify your triggers. Trigger identification quizzes can provide a structured way to recognize when you may be experiencing one of these moments. These quizzes often include questions about your emotional reactions to various situations, helping you identify patterns. This can be combined with useful prompts, such as "Describe a recent situation where you felt intensely emotional. What memories or feelings did it evoke?" Such questions can guide you in exploring and understanding your triggers further.

Reflective Exercise: Identifying Triggers

1. **List Your Triggers**: Write down situations that consistently cause strong emotional reactions.
2. **Reflect on Past Experiences**: Think about similar situations in your past that might be linked to these triggers.

3. **Note Physical Responses**: Document any physical symptoms you notice when triggered.
4. **Explore Emotional Reactions**: Describe the emotions you feel and any memories they bring up.

This exercise can help you gain a deeper understanding of your emotional triggers and their roots. By regularly engaging in such reflective practices, you can become more attuned to your emotional landscape, paving the way for healing and resilience. Don't fear! They get easier with time.

10.2 EXPOSURE THERAPY FOR TRIGGER MANAGEMENT

Exposure therapy is a psychological treatment designed to help you confront and manage your fears by gradually exposing you to the feared objects, activities, or situations in a controlled and safe environment. This approach is particularly effective for reducing sensitivity to emotional triggers, which often stem from past traumas. The underlying principle of exposure therapy is that by facing your fears repeatedly in a safe setting, you can break the cycle of avoidance and reduce the emotional power these triggers hold over you.

When you avoid these triggers, you reinforce the fear and anxiety associated with them. However, by gradually confronting them, you allow your brain to process and integrate the experiences, reducing their emotional impact over time. This method has been shown to be effective for various issues, including phobias, panic disorder, social anxiety, and post-traumatic stress disorder (PTSD).

To conduct exposure therapy safely and effectively, it's crucial to follow a structured, step-by-step approach. Start with gradual exposure techniques, which involve facing your fears in a controlled, step-by-step manner. First, create a hierarchy of triggers, ranking them from least to most distressing. Begin with the least distressing trigger and expose yourself to it repeatedly until your anxiety decreases. For instance, if social situations are a trigger, you might start by imagining yourself in a social setting, then progress to attending a small gathering, and eventually working up to larger events.

While engaging in exposure exercises, it's essential to practice relaxation techniques to manage your anxiety – it's important not to make yourself unnecessarily overwhelmed. Deep breathing, progressive muscle relaxation, and visualization are effective methods to stay calm during exposure. These techniques help you remain grounded and focused, reducing the likelihood of becoming overly nervous or panicking. Over time, as you move up your hierarchy of triggers, you'll find that your emotional responses become less intense, and you gain confidence in your ability to handle these situations.

In the early stages of this method, creating a controlled environment is vital. Choose a quiet, comfortable space where you feel secure. This could be a room in your home or another location where you can focus without distractions. If needed, have a trusted person present to provide support and reassurance. Their presence can offer a sense of safety and help you stay grounded during the exposure exercises. It's important to communicate with this person about your goals and the support you need. The time may come though when you need to move away from this safe space; but this is okay though. It's all part of the process to becoming better.

Consider the story of Alex, who had a debilitating fear of social situations due to past experiences of bullying. By using exposure therapy, he started by imagining himself at a small social gathering. He practiced deep breathing and visualization techniques to stay calm. Gradually, he progressed to attending small get-togethers with friends, then larger events. Over several months, Alex's anxiety decreased significantly, and he regained confidence in social settings.

Another example is Maria, who struggled with the sound of loud voices due to a traumatic experience in her childhood. Her therapist helped her create a hierarchy of triggers, starting with recorded sounds of soft voices and gradually moving to louder, more intense recordings. Throughout the process, Maria practiced relaxation techniques and had her therapist present for support. Eventually, she could handle loud environments without experiencing overwhelming anxiety.

Exposure therapy can be a powerful tool for managing emotional triggers and reclaiming control over your emotional responses. By facing your fears in a structured, safe and supportive environment, you can reduce the emotional impact of your triggers and build resilience. This process requires patience, consistency, and self-compassion, but the benefits of reduced anxiety and increased emotional stability make it a worthwhile endeavor.

10.3 USING MINDFULNESS TO NAVIGATE TRIGGERS

As we've previously come across in this book, mindfulness involves present-moment awareness without judgment. It helps you manage emotions by observing thoughts and feelings without reacting, keeping you grounded and reducing emotional intensity. Fortunately, it offers numerous benefits for emotional regulation and trigger management. By staying present, you can break the automatic loop of reacting to triggers. This awareness creates a space between the trigger and your reaction, giving you the choice to respond more calmly and thoughtfully. Regular mindfulness practice has been shown to decrease anxiety, improve emotional resilience, and enhance overall well-being. It helps you develop a more balanced perspective, enabling you to handle emotional triggers with greater composure and clarity. In fact, all the methods related to mindfulness we've previously mentioned can be beneficial here. Let's summarize some of the uses we've discussed so far:

- Present-moment awareness: Focusing on the here and now without distraction.
- Non-judgmental observation: Observing thoughts and feelings without labeling them as good or bad.
- Acceptance: Allowing emotions and sensations to exist without trying to change them.
- Emotional regulation: Reducing reactivity by staying grounded during emotional distress.

What we'll focus on in this chapter is using the same mindfulness techniques – the body scan, the simple breathing with a focus on the diaphragm – but understood in relation to real-time triggers. For instance, when you notice an emotional response, take a moment to pause and breathe. Label the emotion you are experiencing, such as "anger," "fear," or "sadness." Acknowledge the emotion without judgment, simply observing it. This practice helps you create distance between yourself and the emotion, reducing its intensity. Bring your focus back to the present moment. Use your breath or body sensations as anchors to stay grounded. Remind yourself that the emotion is temporary and will pass. Practice acceptance and let go of negative thoughts, allowing them to dissipate, like dark storm cloud revealing an azure sky.

Mindfulness provides a powerful framework for navigating and managing emotional triggers. By staying present, practicing non-judgmental awareness, and incorporating mindfulness into your daily life, you can develop greater emotional resilience and well-being. It's about building a better relationship with your emotions; putting you in the driving seat and not them.

10.4 DEVELOPING A TRIGGER MANAGEMENT PLAN

Creating a personalized trigger management plan requires a thoughtful approach tailored to your unique needs and experiences. The first step is identifying your key triggers and understanding their impact on your emotional well-being. This involves considering the specific situations, words, or environments that consistently provoke intense emotional reactions. Once you have a clear understanding of your triggers, it's crucial to set specific, achievable goals for managing them. These goals should be realistic and manageable, allowing you to gradually build your confidence and resilience. It's often not entirely productive to say to yourself, "Never again do I want to feel anxious." After all, we can't ask for the moon in such situations; we should think more carefully about what is truly actionable – "I want to feel less nervous when meeting people for the first time."

Implementing your trigger management plan involves practical, incremental steps. Start with manageable triggers that are less overwhelming and gradually build up to more challenging ones. Practicing techniques regularly is vital for building consistency and reinforcing new, healthier patterns of behavior. For instance, if you are working on managing anxiety related to public speaking, begin by practicing relaxation techniques before speaking in front of a small, supportive group. As you become more comfortable, gradually increase the audience size and complexity of the speaking engagements.

It's also important to be flexible and responsive to your needs. Adjust your plan as necessary based on what works and what doesn't. If a particular technique isn't effective, don't be afraid to try something new. The goal is to create a dynamic, adaptable plan that evolves with you.

Keeping a diary containing details about your results allows you to document your experiences, noting what strategies were effective and where you encountered difficulties. Regular self-assessment check-ins help you stay aware of your emotional state and make necessary adjustments to your plan. These check-ins can be weekly or monthly, depending on your preference and your goals. Additionally, seeking feedback from trusted individuals can provide valuable insights and support. Friends, family members, or a therapist can offer perspectives that you may not have considered, helping you tweak your approach.

Building a strong support system is another crucial aspect of managing emotional triggers effectively. Surrounding yourself with individuals who understand your emotional landscape can provide a sense of security and encouragement. Whether it's friends, family, or professional support, having people who can offer perspective, encouragement, and feedback is invaluable. These trusted individuals can help remind you of your progress, offer guidance when you feel stuck, and hold you accountable to your trigger management plan. Additionally, seeking professional guidance from a therapist or counselor can provide structured support and help you deepen your understanding of your emotional patterns, offering you more tailored strategies for coping.

Self-compassion is equally important throughout this process. Managing emotional triggers is often a gradual and challenging journey, and setbacks are a natural part of growth. It's crucial to practice patience and kindness towards yourself as you work through your plan. Instead of focusing on moments where you feel you've fallen short, acknowledge your efforts and celebrate your progress, no matter how small. Cultivating a mindset of self-compassion can prevent feelings of frustration and discouragement, allowing you to stay motivated and committed to the process. Over time, this compassionate approach will help you build resilience, fostering a healthier relationship with your emotions.

By developing a personalized trigger management plan, implementing it with consistency and flexibility, tracking your progress, and building a robust support system, you can take control of your emotional triggers and enhance your emotional well-being. This comprehensive approach empowers you to face your triggers with confidence, resilience, and self-compassion, paving the way for lasting emotional stability and growth.

In the next chapter, we'll explore themes pertaining to support further and look at how to build a supportive community and how to find the right groups and individuals to support your healing journey.

BUILDING A SUPPORTIVE COMMUNITY

I often scroll through social media, but very rarely do I come across incredibly heart-felt posts from people who I know. One evening though, I stumbled upon a post from an old friend sharing her struggles with anxiety. It was raw, honest, and, most importantly, it really struck a chord. The comments section was filled with supportive messages from people who had experienced similar challenges. For the first time, I felt a sense of connection and understanding. While we often think that we'll burden people, if we take the time to open up to them, this is very often not the case. What is much more likely is that we find the answers, the acknowledgement and support that we require within a wider community. As they say, "A problem shared, is a problem halved."

11.1 THE IMPORTANCE OF COMMUNITY IN HEALING

The psychological benefits of being part of a supportive community are immense. When you are surrounded by people who understand and empathize with your experiences, the feelings of isolation and loneliness that often accompany trauma and emotional distress very often begin to fade. This sense of belonging and acceptance is what can likely trigger the starting pistol on the healing process. When you feel like you fit in and are accepted for who you are, it can boost your self-esteem and reinforce your self-worth.

Communities offer a network of support that can be incredibly comforting during tough times. Knowing that there are people you can turn to for help and emotional support provides a safety net that can alleviate stress and anxiety. This support network can also offer practical advice, share resources, and provide encouragement, fostering a sense of resilience. When you are part of a community, you have access to a wealth of shared knowledge and experiences, which can be invaluable in navigating your own challenges. The sad thing is that we often take it for granted when it is constantly around us. Imagine thought for a moment that you move to a completely new place, and you can't even speak the language. Just think about how much information and how many resources you'd lack; then think about the accumulative effect of this over time, the longer you stay there.

Social connections play a vital role in the healing process. Meaningful relationships provide emotional support, which is essential for processing and overcoming trauma. When you share your struggles with empathetic listeners, it validates your experiences and makes you feel less alone. This validation is a powerful antidote to the feelings of shame and self-doubt that often accompany trauma. Additionally, being part of a community offers opportunities for mutual encouragement, where you can both give and receive support, creating a positive feedback loop.

The impact of such communities on mental health is well-documented. Research has shown that individuals with strong social ties are less likely to suffer from depression and anxiety. Studies have demonstrated improved mental health outcomes for those who actively engage in community support. For example, a study published by the National Institutes of Health found that people with strong social connections had a 50% higher survival rate compared to those with weaker social ties. It highlights the sheer importance in belonging, and staving of loneliness.

Personal stories often illustrate these benefits in a relatable way. Take the story of Sarah, who struggled with depression after a painful divorce. She joined a local support group where she met others who had gone through similar experiences. The group's empathy and shared understanding provided Sarah with the emotional support she needed to start her healing process. Over time, the validation and encouragement she received from the group helped her regain her confidence and rebuild her life.

Building trust within a community is essential for creating a safe and supportive environment. Trust is the foundation upon which meaningful relationships are built. One way to build trust is by being consistent in your interactions. Show up regularly, participate actively, and follow through on commitments. Consistency demonstrates reliability and fosters a sense of security within the group. Practicing empathy and active listening is also crucial. When you listen to others with genuine interest and compassion, it shows that you care about their experiences and feelings. This empathy creates a space where people feel safe to share their vulnerabilities.

Encouraging open and honest communication is another key aspect of building trust. Create an environment where people feel comfortable expressing their thoughts and emotions without fear of judgment. This openness allows for deeper connections and creates a sense of community. One way to do this in a support group setting is to set ground rules for respectful communication and confidentiality, all of which can help create a safe and trusting space for all members.

By cultivating these elements—consistency, empathy, and open communication—you can build a supportive community that plays a transformative role in your healing journey. Whether you're dealing with childhood trauma, recovering from toxic relationships, or seeking empowerment through self-awareness, there's strength in numbers!

11.2 FINDING SUPPORT GROUPS AND ONLINE COMMUNITIES

Identifying support groups that align with your needs and interests can take a little work, but is now perhaps easier than ever with the technology we have available at our fingertips. Start by researching local support groups. Many communities have organizations that offer groups for various issues, from childhood trauma to coping with loss. Check bulletin boards at community centers, libraries, or local mental health facilities. Additionally, online directories are invaluable resources. Websites like Mental Health America provide comprehensive lists of support groups categorized by specific issues. Asking for recommendations from therapists, friends, or even colleagues who might have similar experiences can also lead you to valuable resources. It's essential to find a group that resonates with your personal journey and emotional needs.

Not every group is the same, so it can be a good idea to have your own criteria to assess how beneficial it will be for you. After all, group size and dynamics play a significant role in how comfortable you feel sharing your experiences. Smaller groups often provide a more intimate setting, allowing for deeper connections, while larger groups might offer a broader range of perspectives.

The qualifications and experience of the facilitator are also important. A skilled facilitator can create a safe, inclusive environment and guide the group effectively. Ensure that the group's focus aligns with your personal goals. If you're dealing with childhood trauma, find a group specifically tailored to that experience. This alignment ensures that the discussions and support you receive are relevant and beneficial.

Online communities offer a unique platform for emotional support, especially for those who might find it challenging to attend meetings in person at a local pub or cafe. Searching for online forums and social media groups dedicated to mental health can connect you with a global community of individuals who share your experiences. Platforms like Reddit, Facebook, and specialized mental health forums are great starting points. When evaluating online communities, consider the tone and activity level. A supportive, active community is more likely to provide timely responses and a sense of togetherness. Webinars and virtual support sessions can also be incredibly beneficial. These sessions often offer expert insights and allow for real-time interaction which can often prove even more effective than a real get-together.

Just on a side note. Make sure to stay safe when online. Protecting your personal information should always be a priority. Using pseudonyms or anonymous profiles can help maintain your privacy while still allowing you to participate fully. Avoid sharing sensitive details such as your exact location, personal contact information, or anything that could be used to identify you. Most online communities have reporting mechanisms for inappropriate behavior or content. Familiarize yourself with these tools and don't hesitate to use them if you feel uncomfortable or threatened. If you are unfortunate enough to come into contact with a troll, either report them, or just remove yourself – the off switch is always within your grasp!

Case Study: Finding an Online Support Group

Lily, a 32-year-old recovering from a toxic relationship, felt isolated and overwhelmed. She decided to look for an online support group. After researching, she found a Facebook group specifically for individuals recovering from emotional abuse. The group was moderated by a licensed therapist, and the posts were supportive and empathetic. Lily joined the group using an anonymous profile and quickly found herself connecting with others who understood her struggles. She attended weekly virtual meetings and participated in discussions, finding solace in these shared experiences and building friendships at the same time. This community became a crucial part of her healing process, providing her with both emotional support and practical advice.

Finding and participating in support groups and online communities requires effort, but the benefits are well documented. These communities can provide the understanding, validation, and support that are so vital for healing. Whether you choose local groups, online forums, or virtual sessions, connecting with others who share your experiences can significantly enhance your emotional well-being and resilience. It's about finding a space where you feel seen, heard, and supported, making the journey towards healing a shared endeavor.

11.3 BUILDING YOUR PERSONAL SUPPORT NETWORK

Identifying potential members for your personal support network is a fundamental step in fostering a nurturing environment for emotional well-being. Start by considering friends and family members who have consistently shown empathy and understanding for you in the past. These individuals often know you well and can provide a strong foundation of support. Next, think about colleagues and mentors. They can offer valuable perspectives and advice, especially when dealing with work-related stress or seeking professional growth. Neighbors and community members can also be a significant part of your network. These individuals can provide practical support and companionship, making your immediate environment more supportive and inclusive. Unfortunately, the importance of this last group has faded over the last few decades and has increased the loneliness by many who now feel disconnected between themselves and their neighborhood.

Fostering stronger connections with your support network requires regular, meaningful interactions. Begin by scheduling regular check-ins, whether through phone calls, video chats, or face-to-face meetings. These check-ins don't have to be long, it's rather the consistency here that is important. Sharing personal experiences and actively listening to others can deepen these connections. When you share your vulnerabilities and listen to theirs, it builds mutual trust and understanding. Expressing gratitude and appreciation is another powerful way to strengthen these bonds. A simple "thank you" or a note of appreciation can go a long way in showing that you value their support and presence in your life.

Communicating your needs clearly and respectfully is essential for maintaining a healthy support network. Using "I" statements, as we've previously discussed, can help express your needs without sounding accusatory. For example, say, "I feel overwhelmed and could use some help," instead of "You never help me." This approach fosters understanding and minimizes defensiveness. Setting boundaries respectfully is equally important. Be honest about what you can and cannot handle, and communicate this clearly to your support network. For instance, if you need alone time to recharge, let them know. Asking for specific types of support can also make a significant difference. Whether you need someone to listen, offer advice, or help with tasks, being specific helps others understand how they can best provide that support to you.

Maintaining a balanced support network involves ensuring diversity in the types of support you receive. Emotional support is crucial, but practical and informational support can be equally valuable. While a friend might take more time to listen to you carefully, a mentor can offer career advice, and a neighbor might assist with day-to-day tasks. Avoiding over-reliance on any one person is important to prevent being overbearing and maintain healthy relationships. Regularly reassessing and adjusting your network ensures that it continues to meet your evolving needs. This might involve seeking new connections or reevaluating existing ones to ensure they remain supportive and beneficial.

Reflecting on my own experience, I remember a time when I felt completely overwhelmed by the demands of work and personal life. I reached out to different people in my network for various forms of support. My best friend provided emotional comfort, my mentor offered practical advice on managing work stress, and my neighbor helped with some practical things I needed – like clearing up the leaves from the driveway. This diverse support system made a significant difference, allowing me to navigate through that challenging period more effectively.

In the process of building your support network, it's also important to be open and realize the potential that new connections can offer. Attend community events, join clubs or groups that interest you, and be willing to step out of your comfort zone to meet new people. Sometimes, support can come from unexpected places, and being open to new relationships can enrich your network further. Remember, the goal is to create a web of support that is strong, diverse, and adaptable to your changing needs. By investing time and effort into building and nurturing these connections, you lay the foundation for a more resilient and supportive environment that can significantly enhance your emotional well-being.

11.4 PARTICIPATING IN COMMUNITY HEALING ACTIVITIES

Participating in community healing activities offers numerous benefits that can significantly enhance your emotional well-being. When you engage with like-minded individuals, you build connections that can provide a sense of belonging and mutual understanding. Sharing experiences in a supportive environment allows you to learn from others, gaining new perspectives and coping strategies. These activities also provide access to collective resources, such as information about local therapists, self-help books, or workshops that you might not have discovered on your own. The shared support system within these communities fosters resilience, helping you navigate your healing process with the backing of a strong network.

Community healing activities come in various forms, each offering unique benefits. Group therapy sessions are a structured way to explore your emotions and experiences in a safe, guided environment. These sessions are often led by a licensed therapist who can provide professional insights and facilitate meaningful discussions. Community workshops and seminars on topics like mindfulness, self-compassion, or cognitive behavioral techniques offer opportunities to learn new skills and practices. Healing circles and support groups provide a more intimate setting where members can share their stories and offer mutual support. Volunteer opportunities and community service can also be adopted. Helping others can give a profound sense of purpose and fulfillment, and it often leads to connections with people who share similar values.

Finding local healing activities within your community requires a bit of research but it can be the start of something wonderful. Start by checking community bulletin boards at local libraries, community centers, or coffee shops. These often have flyers and announcements for upcoming events and groups. Also, don't forget to go online. Websites like Eventbrite or Meetup allow you to search for local events based on your interests. Don't hesitate to ask for recommendations from local organizations, such as mental health clinics, religious institutions, or even friends and family. They might know of groups or activities that align with your needs. Engaging in these activities can open doors to new relationships and resources that support your healing journey.

Once you find a community activity that resonates with you, take it upon yourself to make the most out of it. Attend regularly and make a commitment to participate fully. Consistency helps build trust and deepen connections within the group. Offering support to others in the group can also be incredibly rewarding. Whether it's lending a listening ear, sharing helpful resources, or simply offering words of encouragement, your contributions can make a significant impact. Sharing your personal experiences and insights can lead to a reciprocal relationship where everyone benefits from the collective wisdom of the group. These interactions not only support your healing but also enrich the community as a whole.

Reflection Section: Finding Your Community Healing Activity

1. **List Your Interests and Needs**: Write down what you're looking for in a community. Is it emotional support, learning new skills, or finding like-minded individuals?

2. **Research Local Options**: Use online directories, community bulletin boards, and recommendations from friends or local organizations to find activities that match your interests.

3. **Attend and Reflect**: Try out a few different activities. After each one, reflect on how it made you feel. Did you feel supported? Did you learn something new? Did you connect with others?

4. **Commit and Engage**: Once you find an activity that resonates with you, commit to attending regularly. Engage fully, offer support to others, and share your experiences. You may soon be the person helping to recruit the next members!

Engaging in community healing activities not only provides emotional support but also ensures a sense of belonging and purpose. These activities offer a platform to share experiences, learn from others, and access a wealth of resources and knowledge. Whether through group therapy, workshops, support groups, or volunteer work, these communal efforts contribute significantly to your healing process. As you immerse yourself in these activities, you'll find that the connections you build and the support you receive will help you navigate your healing journey with greater resilience and hope.

With these strategies in place, you're well-equipped to build a robust support network and get participating with those who surround you. The next, and final, chapter will delve into creating a sustainable healing journey, ensuring that the progress you make is both meaningful and enduring.

CREATING A SUSTAINABLE HEALING JOURNEY

I've tried many times to implement a lot of what is covered in this book, but as with so many things – it's easier said than done. Over time, it's occurred to me that there must be some systems in place, some structure to help a person stay on the right track to getting better. It's all well and good giving the advice, but we need plans to make sure that it is stuck to. Without a clear roadmap, it is easy to feel lost and overwhelmed. And, as always, this is a personal thing – it has to be created specifically to meet your individual requirements. With this in mind, this chapter aims to guide you in developing a sustainable and personalized healing plan, ensuring that your efforts are both meaningful and effective in both the short term and the long term. Let's get going!

12.1 DEVELOPING A PERSONALIZED HEALING PLAN

Understanding that your healing journey is unique is the first step. Each person's experiences, challenges, and strengths are different, and so too must be their approach to healing. Begin by conducting a thorough self-assessment to identify your emotional triggers and challenges. Consider the specific events or situations that cause you distress and note any patterns. Reflect on your past healing efforts and evaluate their effectiveness. What worked well? What didn't? This reflection will provide valuable insights into your personal strengths and areas that need growth.

Setting realistic and achievable goals is essential for maintaining motivation and seeing progress. Use the SMART (Specific, Measurable, Achievable, Relevant, Time-bound) framework, something we've already covered in detail in previous chapters, to create clear and actionable goals. For instance, if you aim to reduce anxiety, a SMART goal could be: "I will practice mindfulness meditation for 10 minutes each morning for the next 30 days." Breaking down larger goals into smaller, manageable steps makes them less daunting and more attainable. Prioritize your goals based on immediate needs and long-term vision, ensuring that each step you take is purposeful and aligned with your overall healing journey.

Choosing appropriate healing practices involves exploring various therapeutic approaches and self-care practices that resonate with you. Experimentation is key here. You might find that Cognitive Behavioral Therapy (CBT) helps you reframe negative thoughts, while mindfulness practices keep you grounded in the present. Art therapy might offer a creative outlet for expressing emotions that are hard to verbalize. Incorporate self-care practices like regular exercise, balanced nutrition, and adequate sleep to support your overall well-being. Seeking professional guidance from therapists or counselors can provide tailored support and additional resources to enhance your healing journey.

Creating a record of your healing plan is essential for monitoring your progress and making any needed changes. Use a dedicated journal or planner to outline your goals, strategies, and daily practices, or opt for an online version using whatever resources you have to hand to make it a fun process; add color and pictures if you think it'll help. Create a visual roadmap or mind map to see the bigger picture and how each element of your plan connects. Setting regular review dates allows you to assess your progress, reflect on what's working, and make adjustments as needed. This documentation serves as both a guide and a record of your journey, helping you stay organized and focused.

Self-Assessment Exercise: Discovering Your Unique Healing Needs

Use the summarized information below as a quick guide to get yourself going.

1. **Identify Emotional Triggers and Challenges**: List situations or events that cause you significant emotional distress. Note any physical reactions and emotional responses.
2. **Reflect on Past Healing Efforts**: Write about previous attempts at healing. What strategies did you use? What were the outcomes?
3. **Recognize Personal Strengths and Areas for Growth**: Identify your strengths and how they can support your healing. Acknowledge areas where you need more support or development.
4. **Set SMART Goals**: Use the SMART framework to create specific, measurable, achievable, relevant, and time-bound goals for your healing journey.
5. **Choose Healing Practices**: Explore different therapeutic approaches and self-care practices. Write down which ones resonate with you and how you plan to incorporate them into your daily routine.

This personalized approach ensures that your healing journey is tailored to your unique needs and goals. By setting realistic goals, choosing appropriate healing practices, and documenting your progress, you can create a sustainable plan that supports long-term growth and emotional resilience.

12.2 MAINTAINING CONSISTENCY IN YOUR HEALING PRACTICES

Establishing a routine is what makes all of these techniques transformative; without it, we might as well be spinning in circles. After all, routine creates a sense of stability and predictability, which is particularly beneficial when you're dealing with the unpredictability of emotions. Set aside dedicated time each day for your healing activities. This could be as simple as a morning meditation session or an evening journaling practice. Incorporate these activities into your daily habits so they become second nature. For instance, you might start your day with a few minutes of mindfulness meditation before breakfast and end your day by journaling about your experiences. Using reminders and alarms can help you stay on track. Set an alarm for your meditation time or a reminder to journal before bed. These small steps create a structured environment that supports your healing.

Obstacles to consistency are common but manageable. It's crucial to identify potential distractions and find solutions. If you know that your mornings are hectic, try scheduling your healing activities for a quieter time of day. Creating a supportive environment also fosters consistency. Surround yourself with items that remind you of your goals—perhaps a vision board or a dedicated space for your healing practices. Practicing self-compassion and being flexible is essential when setbacks occur. Life is unpredictable, and some days you might miss a meditation session or forget to journal. Instead of being harsh on yourself, acknowledge the setback and gently guide yourself back to your routine the next day.

Staying motivated and engaged in your healing practices can be challenging, but there are strategies to help. Setting short-term milestones and rewarding progress is an effective way to maintain motivation. Celebrate small victories, like completing a week of daily meditation or successfully managing a trigger. Finding inspiration through books, podcasts, and role models can also keep you engaged. Surround yourself with positive influences and stories of others who have successfully navigated their healing journeys. Connect with a supportive community for encouragement. Online forums, support groups, or even a close friend can provide the motivation and reassurance you need to stay committed (refer back to Chapter 11 for more advice on this).

As well as tracking progress though a journal or through the many apps which are available, seeking feedback from trusted individuals or therapists can offer valuable perspectives on your progress. They can provide encouragement, suggest adjustments, and help you stay focused on your goals. If you're struggling, it's really okay to ask for help. It's something I had to learn the hard way and is something I wish I'd learnt when I was much younger.

Interactive Exercise: Creating Your Consistent Healing Routine

Use the key information below to focus on *how* you will stay motivated.

1. **Identify Daily Healing Activities**: List the activities that you find most beneficial, such as meditation, journaling, or exercise.

2. **Schedule Dedicated Time**: Decide when you will perform these activities each day. Consider your daily schedule and choose times that are realistic and sustainable.

3. **Set Reminders and Alarms**: Use your phone or an alarm clock to set reminders for your healing activities. This will help you stay consistent.

4. **Create a Supportive Environment**: Designate a space in your home for your healing practices. Fill it with items that inspire and comfort you.

5. **Plan for Obstacles**: Think about potential distractions or challenges and develop strategies to overcome them. For example, if mornings are busy, schedule your activities for the evening.

6. **Track Your Progress**: Use a journal or app to document your daily activities, reflections, and progress. Review your entries regularly to stay motivated and make necessary adjustments. Or, alternatively, work alongside a professional; never fear asking for help if you require it.

By establishing a fixed routine, overcoming obstacles, staying motivated, and tracking your progress, you create a solid foundation for your healing practices. This approach ensures that your efforts are consistent, meaningful, and, most importantly, effective.

12.3 ADAPTING YOUR PLAN AS YOU GROW

Recognizing the need for change is a vital aspect of maintaining a sustainable healing plan. It's important to remain flexible and responsive to your evolving needs. As you progress, you may see signs that your current plan may no longer be as effective as it once was. Perhaps the strategies that once brought comfort now feel stale, or you find yourself facing new challenges that your existing plan doesn't factor in. Reflecting on these new challenges and opportunities for growth allows you to stay attuned to your healing needs. Be open to exploring new practices that might resonate more deeply with where you are now. For instance, if you've been focusing on mindfulness, but find it less impactful, you might explore art therapy or a new form of exercise.

Incorporating new insights and techniques into your healing plan keeps it dynamic and effective. Continuous learning and adaptation are the buzz-words here. Attending workshops and seminars can introduce you to fresh perspectives and techniques that you might not have considered. Reading books and articles on new therapeutic approaches can provide valuable insights and practical strategies. Consulting with therapists or coaches can offer tailored advice and new angles on your healing. These activities not only enrich your plan but also keep you engaged and motivated. For example, learning about the latest advancements in CBT might offer new tools for managing anxiety, while a seminar on trauma-informed yoga could introduce a new, healing physical practice. Psychology, in general, is a vast and rich area filled with nuance; very often, it's exciting and beneficial to read up on the latest insights.

Balancing structure and flexibility in your healing plan is key. Maintaining core practices, such as daily mindfulness or regular therapy sessions, provides a stable foundation. At the same time, experimenting with new practices and adjusting them based on your experiences ensures that your plan remains fresh and effective. Creating a flexible schedule that accommodates these changes can help you integrate new practices without feeling overwhelmed. You might maintain your morning meditation routine but add a weekly art therapy session to explore creativity and emotional expression. This balance allows for consistency while also embracing the need for innovation and growth.

Reflecting on personal growth is an ongoing process that helps you stay connected to your progress and the effectiveness of your healing plan. Regularly journaling about your personal achievements and challenges provides a space for self-reflection. Note the emotional and behavioral changes you've experienced, and how these shifts have impacted your daily life. Celebrating progress, no matter how small, reinforces your commitment to healing. Setting new goals based on your reflections keeps your plan dynamic and relevant. Let's give an example. If you've successfully managed to form a new friendship, when previously you struggled to connect with people in the new town you moved to, give yourself a pat on the back – write down exactly what this achievement means to you. This cycle of reflection and goal-setting ensures that your healing journey is always moving forward, adapting to your needs, and fostering continuous growth.

Reflection Exercise: Adapting Your Healing Plan

Let's summarize below, and make sure we have all the key information to hand.

1. **Identify Signs of Ineffectiveness**: Reflect on any feelings of stagnation or new challenges that your current plan doesn't address.
2. **Explore New Practices**: List new therapeutic approaches or self-care practices you're curious about.
3. **Attend Workshops and Read**: Find a workshop or book that introduces a new technique or perspective.
4. **Consult Experts**: Schedule a session with a therapist or coach to gain fresh insights.
5. **Balance Structure and Flexibility**: Maintain your core practices while experimenting with new ones. Adjust your schedule to fit these changes.

6. **Journal Regularly**: Document your achievements and challenges. Reflect on emotional and behavioral changes.
7. **Set New Goals**: Based on your reflections, set new, relevant goals to continue your growth.

12.4 CELEBRATING YOUR HEALING MILESTONES

Celebrating your healing milestones is an enthralling part of the whole process. It's not just about acknowledging the big achievements, but also recognizing the small steps that get you there. Celebrating these moments can boost your motivation and reinforce the positive behaviors that contribute to your healing. When you take a moment to appreciate your achievements, you not only build self-esteem and confidence but also reinforce your commitment to your healing journey. This acknowledgment helps you see how far you've come, making the road ahead feel more manageable and the progress tangible.

Identifying significant milestones in your healing process is crucial for celebrating appropriately. Start by reflecting on the initial goals you set and the progress you've made towards them. Recognize the behavioral and emotional changes you've achieved, such as setting a healthy boundary or being more open and communicative in your relationships. These recognitions provide a clear picture of your growth, fostering a sense of accomplishment and encouraging further progress.

There are many creative ways to celebrate your milestones, catering to different preferences. Treating yourself to a special activity or experience that you enjoy can be incredibly rewarding. This could be a spa day to relax, a nature hike to reconnect with yourself, or a special meal at your favorite restaurant. Creating a visual representation of your progress can also be powerful. Consider making a vision board or an achievement collage that you can look at to remind yourself of how far you've come. Sharing your milestones with a supportive community or loved ones can amplify the joy and provide additional encouragement. Whether it's a small gathering with friends or a post on social media, sharing your achievements can generate a sense of connection with others and a collective understanding and witnessing of your moving forward.

Continuing the journey involves using these celebrations as motivation to keep moving forward. Set new goals and challenges that build on your achievements. Reflect on your overall progress and plan for the future. This reflection helps you stay focused on your growth and maintain a positive, growth-oriented mindset. Remember that, when all is said and done, celebrating milestones is more about reinforcing the behaviors and practices that have brought you this far; use these moments to fuel your determination and commitment to your ongoing healing journey.

So, in essence, celebrating your healing milestones is a powerful way to acknowledge your progress, build confidence, and stay motivated. Whether through special activities, visual representations, or sharing with others, these celebrations provide tangible reminders of your growth. Keep setting new goals, reflecting on your journey, and maintaining a positive outlook.

SHARE THE POWER OF HEALING

The stronger you become and the more you commit to your healing journey, the more likely it is that you'll want to help other people out on the same path. Here's a chance for you to do that now.

Simply by sharing your honest opinion of this book and a little about your own experience, you'll inspire new readers to begin their own work on reparenting their inner child, and you'll show them exactly where they can find all the guidance they need to get started.

WANT TO HELP OTHERS?

Thank you so much for your support. There's a bright future ahead of you—and your journey towards it starts right now.

Scan the QR code below

CONCLUSION

As we come to the close of our journey together, let's revisit the heart of this book. "Healing and Reparenting Your Inner Child" was born from a vision to empower you to heal from childhood trauma, break free from negative patterns, and build emotional resilience. Through a blend of Cognitive Behavioral Therapy (CBT), mindfulness, and self-compassion, this book aimed to provide practical tools to help you grow and build on your emotional well-being.

At the core of our exploration lies the concept of the inner child and how both understanding it and then through healing it we can really achieve wonderful piece of mind. This part of you holds the memories, emotions, and behaviors from your childhood which continue to influence your adult life. By acknowledging and nurturing your inner child, you can address the many unresolved patterns of negative behavior that have carried themselves through to the present moment – adulthood, middle-age or even retirement. Recognizing and addressing the wounded inner child is the foundation of your healing journey that this book has set out to accomplish.

Cultivating self-compassion and self-love has been a vital part of this journey. We explored various methods, including daily affirmations, meditations, and techniques to overcome self-blame. We spoke at length about how these practices can help you to treat yourself with the kindness and understanding you deserve, propelling you forward to have a healthier relationship with yourself.

Practical exercises for healing, such as journaling prompts, guided visualization, creating safe spaces, and art therapy, have provided you with tangible tools to engage actively in your healing process. These exercises are designed to help you release pent-up emotions, gain clarity, and best utilize your own form of self-expression.

Rewiring negative thought patterns through CBT, affirmations, and mindfulness practices has been another key component. Identifying and replacing negative thoughts with more positive and realistic ones is essential for breaking free from destructive mental habits. Although this process can be lengthy, I hope the book has given you a warm welcome into some of the theory that lies behind the practice.

Emotional regulation techniques, including mindfulness-based stress reduction, breathing exercises, and grounding techniques, aimed to equip you with strategies to manage your emotions and triggers effectively. These tools, when harnessed effectively, will help you to stay centered and calm, even in challenging situations.

We talked about strategies to rebuild trust in relationships, enhance communication, establish boundaries, and embrace vulnerability. These skills are crucial for nurturing stronger, more authentic connections with others. By consistently practicing them, we can create healthier and more fulfilling relationships.

The process needed to break generational trauma has been a significant focus throughout this book. By identifying and interrupting these patterns, you can create a positive legacy for future generations. This process involves recognizing inherited emotional patterns and actively working to break them. We discussed how this, in many ways, can bring your family together, and how it is a chance to tell those, as yet, untold stories.

A key focus of this journey has also been cultivating self-awareness and personal growth through various exercises designed to deepen self-understanding, uncover core beliefs, and strengthen a sense of personal empowerment. These practices have served as the bedrock for transformative change, as self-awareness is the essential foundation for all personal growth. By continually engaging in this process, we create the opportunity to align our actions with our true values and unlock our full potential, making lasting growth possible.

Furthermore, we discussed a range of therapeutic approaches, including CBT, Jungian theory, and regression therapy, and how combinations of these can create a well-rounded healing framework. By blending these methods, we take a more holistic approach to healing, addressing multiple dimensions of trauma and emotional wounds. This integrated strategy allows for a deeper exploration of the unconscious mind while also offering practical tools for managing current emotional challenges, ultimately promoting more profound and lasting recovery.

We emphasized the importance of navigating and managing emotional triggers through self-awareness, exposure therapy, and mindfulness, which empower individuals to take control of their emotional responses. By recognizing and addressing these triggers, one can significantly enhance emotional stability, paving the way for healthier interactions and a more balanced life.

Later on in the book, we also highlighted the necessity of building a supportive community as a crucial component of the healing journey. Engaging with support groups, establishing personal support networks, and participating in community healing activities fosters the encouragement and connection essential for thriving in recovery.

Finally, we developed the concept of creating a sustainable healing journey by crafting a personalized healing plan, maintaining consistency, adapting to challenges, and celebrating milestones. These key steps ensure that healing efforts remain meaningful and effective, ultimately leading to profound personal transformation and long-lasting well-being.

I urge you to continue practicing the exercises and techniques you've learned in this book. Healing is a continuous process, and regular practice will help you maintain and enhance your progress. If you need additional support, don't hesitate to seek professional help from therapists or counselors; they are there for this reason.

I cannot begin to emphasize enough how joining a supportive community or support group can provide you with mutual encouragement and overwhelming support. Sharing your journey with others who understand can be incredibly validating and empowering. Speak to your friends, your family; that is what they are there for.

Commit to self-compassion. Be kind and patient with yourself as you navigate your healing journey. Remember, you are worthy of love and understanding, especially from yourself; that, many would say, is why you are here – to learn how to be compassionate to yourself, and so, in turn, to others.

I want to leave you with an empowering message: you possess incredible strength and resilience. Healing is a journey, and by taking the steps outlined in this book, you are reclaiming your emotional freedom and creating a brighter, more fulfilling future. Keep moving forward, and remember that you are not alone on this path. You possess the tools, the wisdom, and the unwavering support to not just survive, but to truly thrive.

REFERENCES

Inner Child Work: How Your Past Shapes Your Present https://www.verywellmind.com/inner-child-work-how-your-past-shapes-your-present-7152929

The Wounded Inner Child | CPTSDfoundation.org https://cptsdfoundation.org/2020/07/13/the-wounded-inner-child/

Reflections on Alice Miller https://www.psychologytoday.com/us/blog/suffer-the-children/202104/reflections-alice-miller

Neuroplasticity and Childhood Trauma: Effects, Healing, ... https://psychcentral.com/ptsd/the-roles-neuroplasticity-and-emdr-play-in-healing-from-childhood-trauma

The Role of Self-Compassion in Development: A Healthier ... https://www.ncbi.nlm.nih.gov/pmc/articles/PMC2790748/

How to Effectively Write Affirmations and Practice Them + ... https://blog.gratefulness.me/how-to-write-affirmations-how-to-do-affirmations/

Self-Compassion Practices: Cultivate Inner Peace and Joy https://self-compassion.org/self-compassion-practices/

Tackling Self-Blame and Self-Criticism: 5 Strategies to Try https://www.psychologytoday.com/us/blog/tech-support/201801/tackling-self-blame-and-self-criticism-5-strategies-to-try

Journaling About Trauma and Stress Can Heal Your Body https://www.psychologytoday.com/us/blog/prescriptions-life/201912/journaling-about-trauma-and-stress-can-heal-your-body

Guided Imagery in Therapy: 20 Powerful Scripts and ... https://positivepsychology.com/guided-imagery-scripts/

Creating a Safe Space for the Wounded Inner Child https://www.lindanardelli.com/creating-a-safe-space-for-the-wounded-inner-child/

Trauma-Informed Approaches to Expressive Arts Therapy https://cars-rp.org/_MHTTC/docs/Expressive-Arts-Therapy-Toolkit.pdf

Cognitive Distortions: 22 Examples & Worksheets (& PDF) https://positivepsychology.com/cognitive-distortions/

Negative Thoughts – Self-Monitoring Record https://www.psychologytools.com/resource/negative-thoughts-self-monitoring-record/

Cognitive Restructuring: Techniques and Examples https://www.healthline.com/health/cognitive-restructuring

Mindfulness for Your Health https://newsinhealth.nih.gov/2021/06/mindfulness-your-health

How to Identify and Manage Your Emotional Triggers https://www.healthline.com/health/mental-health/emotional-triggers

Health Benefits of Mindfulness-Based Stress Reduction https://www.verywellmind.com/benefits-of-mindfulness-based-stress-reduction-88861

Breathing Techniques for Stress Relief https://www.webmd.com/balance/stress-management/stress-relief-breathing-techniques

30 Grounding Techniques to Quiet Distressing Thoughts https://www.healthline.com/health/grounding-techniques

Childhood maltreatment is associated with distrust and ... https://www.ncbi.nlm.nih.gov/pmc/articles/PMC7856450/

Rebuilding Trust in Yourself After Trauma https://rcchicago.org/rebuilding-trust-in-yourself-after-trauma/

7 Keys to Effective Communication Skills in Relationships https://seattlechristiancounseling.com/articles/7-keys-to-effective-communication-skills-in-relationships

Establishing and maintaining personal boundaries are crucial steps in asserting your needs and preserving your emotional well-being. Boundaries enable you to navigate relationships in a way that respects both your own and others' autonomy, fostering a sense of self-awareness and independence.

Generational trauma is a form of psychological distress that is passed down from one generation to the next. Individuals within a family may inherit unresolved emotional wounds, leading them to experience various physical or psychological symptoms without directly encountering the initial traumatic event.

Intergenerational transmission of trauma effects https://www.ncbi.nlm.nih.gov/pmc/articles/PMC6127768/

Uncovering the Biological Basis of Intergenerational Trauma https://physicianfocus.nyulangone.org/uncovering-the-biological-basis-of-intergenerational-trauma/

Using Mindfulness Techniques in Trauma Therapy Sessions https://renewedwellnesscounseling.com/using-mindfulness-techniques-in-trauma-therapy-sessions/

Emotional Self-Awareness: The Cornerstone of ... https://rm.edu/blog/emotional-self-awareness-the-cornerstone-of-emotional-intelligence/

Mindfulness: The Key to Self-Awareness https://brizomagazine.com/2019/11/18/mindfulness-the-key-to-self-awareness/

2 Strategies for Uncovering Limiting Beliefs https://thinkgrowprosper.com/blog/2017/5/10/uncovering-limiting-beliefs

Master SMART Goals for Personal Development + Examples https://www.briefblink.com/smart-goals-for-personal-development/

Inner Child Healing: 35 Practical Tools for Growing Beyond ... https://positivepsychology.com/inner-child-healing/

Inner Child Work: The Path to Healing Through Self-Reparenting The notion of the "inner child" plays a pivotal role in various therapeutic frameworks, including Transactional Analysis and Gestalt. This concept underscores the deep-seated emotional experiences and patterns established during childhood, which continue to influence behavior and emotional responses in adulthood. Engaging in inner child work involves a compassionate return to these early experiences, offering a chance to address unresolved trauma, heal emotional wounds, and alter negative patterns of behavior. Through the process of self-reparenting, individuals learn to provide for themselves the care, validation, and love they might have lacked, fostering a nurturing environment for healing and growth. This transformative journey empowers one to rebuild emotional resilience, cultivate self-love, and embrace a future unburdened by the past's shadows.

Regression Therapy: Uses, Types, and Techniques https://www.verywellhealth.com/regressive-hypnosis-therapy-5270347

Integrative Therapy: Definition, Techniques, & Examples https://positivepsychology.com/integrative-therapy/

What Are Triggers, and How Do They Form? https://psychcentral.com/lib/what-is-a-trigger

How to Identify and Manage Your Emotional Triggers https://www.healthline.com/health/mental-health/emotional-triggers

What Is Exposure Therapy? Exposure therapy is a therapeutic practice designed to help individuals confront their fears. By facing the very things they have been avoiding, this approach encourages individuals to gradually reduce their fear and minimize avoidance behaviors.

Mindfulness and Emotion Regulation: Insights from ... https://www.ncbi.nlm.nih.gov/pmc/articles/PMC5337506/

The Importance of Community and Mental Health https://www.nami.org/Blogs/NAMI-Blog/November-2019/The-Importance-of-Community-and-Mental-Health

The Connection Prescription: Using the Power of Social ... https://www.ncbi.nlm.nih.gov/pmc/articles/PMC6125010/

Find Support Groups https://www.mhanational.org/find-support-groups

5 Ways to Constitute Safety in Your Online Community https://www.grazitti.com/blog/5-ways-to-constitute-safety-in-your-online-community/

Trauma Recovery: Stages and 7 Things to Consider https://www.healthline.com/health/mental-health/trauma-recovery

How to Set and Use SMART Goals https://www.verywellmind.com/smart-goals-for-lifestyle-change-2224097

The Essential Role of Consistency in Therapy https://www.houstonfamilypsychology.com/blog/2024/4/16/title-the-essential-role-of-consistency-in-therapy-building-bridges-to-mental-wellness

The Importance of Celebrating Milestones in Recovery https://www.wellbrookrecovery.com/post/importance-of-celebrating-milestones-in-recovery

Alexa Vicktoria. "80 Healing Inner Child Quotes to Feel Validated." Ambitiously Alexa. Last modified September 18, 2023. https://ambitiouslyalexa.com/healing-inner-child-quotes/

"How to Heal Your Inner Child." Lumo Health. Last modified October 17, 2024. https://www.lumohealth.care/blog/do-you-have-a-wounded-inner-child-here-are-7-key-signs

www.ingramcontent.com/pod-product-compliance
Lightning Source LLC
Chambersburg PA
CBHW032055040426
42335CB00037B/718